T0114046

A TALE OF TWO BROTHERS

The Story Of The Wright Brothers

ORVILLE WRIGHT

WILBUR WRIGHT

JUDITH A. DEMPSEY

Order this book online at www.trafford.com
or email orders@trafford.com

Most Trafford titles are also available at major online book retailers.

Print information available on the last page.

ISBN: 978-1-4120-0146-5 (sc)
ISBN: 978-1-4122-1116-1 (e)

Trafford rev. 10/08/2016

www.trafford.com
North America & international
toll-free: 1 888 232 4444 (USA & Canada)
fax: 812 355 4082

CONTENTS

••

PICTURE CREDITS

"Courtesy of Special Collections and Archives, Wright State University" pages: 7, 9, 41, 44, 44, 49, 59, 61, 70, 75, 87, 94, 110, 114, 117, 121, 128, 143, 158, and Wilbur, Orville and the 1902 glider on the cover.

"Courtesy of the Library of Congress" pages: 13, 16, 22, 29, 36, 50, 52, 142, 144, 146 and the title page.

"Outer Banks History Center, Manteo, NC, Courtesy of the National Park Service, Wright Brothers National Memorial" pages: 154, 155, 156, and 157.

"Image courtesy of Earth Sciences and Image Analysis Laboratory, NASA Johnson Space Center" (http://col.jsc.nasa.gov), *The Blue Marble,* page 2.

"Courtesy of National Air and Space Museum, Smithsonian Institution" page 3 (NASM No. 2B-31409) [SIA-38387-A], page 4 (NASM No. 2B-31406) [SI A-38388-A], page 135 (NASM No. 2B-31188) [SI A-32497-A].

The Wright Memorial on the front and back covers was photographed by Jack Dempsey.

The 1902 glider on the front cover was the glider in which the Wrights' achieved for "the first time control over all three flight motions; wing warping for roll control, [the] elevator [forward rudder] for pitch control and a single vertical rudder for yaw control (Young and Fitzgerald 45).

Positive responses for quoting from other publications have been received from:

The University of North Carolina Press:

Dover Publications Inc.;

John Blair Publisher;

McGraw Hill.

The following credit lines were requested.

THE OUTER BANKS OF NORTH CAROLINA, 1584 -1958 by David Stick. Copyright 1958 by David Stick; renewed 1986 Published by the University of North Carolina Press. Used by permission of the publisher.

Fred Kelly. The Wright Brothers: Dover Publications

Fred Howard. Wilbur and Orville Wright: A Biography of the Wright Brothers: Dover Publications

FOREWORD

As we come to the end of the first one hundred years of powered flight, the story of the Wright brothers and the first flight will continue to inspire generations to come to achieve the impossible. Judith A. Dempsey has captured the compelling story of Wilbur and Orville Wright's conquest of the air. Their story is timeless. Aviation is part of our national heritage. It has made America the world's most powerful force for global change. It is mankind's greatest tool in our quest for knowledge in a greater frontier.

I am still excited about flying on an airplane. The wonder of flight is still a miracle to me. I have just returned from a trip to Australia. We started from the East Coast of America, flew to the West Coast and then flew fifteen more hours across the great Pacific Ocean. Less than seventy years ago, this twenty-three hour flight would have taken months by ship. If it weren't for a little turbulence now and then, you would think you were floating on a cloud.

A couple of years back, I had an opportunity to get a back seat ride in the F-15E "Strike Eagle", the Air Force's most superior fighter jet. The hour-and-a-half flight was much more thrilling and stimulating than the flight to Australia. The high performance take-off from the airstrip – climbing vertical to 14,000 feet before we reached the end of the runway - was the ride of a lifetime.

The solitude and exhilaration of these two adventures are something Wilbur and Orville Wright could have never imagined possible. The airplane has succeeded beyond their wildest dreams. In 1929, Orville wrote, "Aviation has gone beyond my dreams." Flight has become old hat to hundreds of millions of people to the point where it is almost impossible for us to imagine our world without it. The fundamental principles discovered and developed by the Wright brothers laid the foundation for the first generation of flight, which has traveled from Kitty Hawk to the moon within the lifetime of a human being.

Judith A. Dempsey with her eloquent writing style has captured the essence of the Wright brothers' achievements. Their loving family - a mother, father, sister, and older brothers – were the backbone behind their success. I think you will enjoy reading this book.

Darrell Collins, Historian, Wright Brothers National Memorial
Kitty Hawk, North Carolina
March 12, 2003

Preface

Whoever would have predicted that two brothers, Wilbur and Orville Wright, neither of whom had graduated from high school, would turn the work of experts upside down and by their own research and experimentati on conquer the air? Yet, that is exactly what happened. They made their impossible dream come true.

Having been raised in Ohio, I was vaguely aware that the Wright brothers were two Ohioans who had created the first airplane to fly successfully. I must admit that my knowledge about them or their achievement really didn't expand much beyond that until 1989 when I moved to the Outer Banks of North Carolina, the site of the world's first manned, powered flight. After several years of seeing the Wright memorial there and taking visitors to the National Memorial site, both my fascination and admiration for these two men from my home state grew until I realized their story was one that could inspire others to dream, too.

During my years as an educator I have bee n keenly aware that we often fail to focus attention on creditable role models, but instead focus on the lives of movie stars and sports figures, thus limiting the vision of what our lives might become. My purpose in writing *A Tale of Two Brothers* was to concentrate on the human side of the Wright story, hoping that readers, young and old, might see the many possibilities in their own lives and set goals to make these a reality, as the Wright brothers did.

The story of the Wright brothers contains many pos sible themes such as their personal lives, their contributions to aeronautical engineering, the dangers of early flight, the difficulties of the aviation business, patent infringements and litigation, and the competition among the early pioneers in flight to gain recognition. I have chosen to tell their story focusing on the chronology of their personal lives as much as possible, as well as giving basic attention to the other themes. Photographs are used to illustrate the text and to give better understanding to the reader. The Wrights documented their early accomplishments using the photographic methods of the times. It has been difficult limiting the number of the photographs because they add so much to the story.

What the Wright brothers accomplished was a monumental breakthrough in the field of aviation. Although I describe the basics of their scientific work, my principal focus is on the human dimension of their story. I was looking not only for the facts but the feelings. How did they come to be the pe ople they became? What was their relationship to each other? What was the basis of the choices they made? Why did they make the choices they did?

Whenever possible the words of Orville or Wilbur are used to explain their own work. Both of the Wrights und erstood and described their work with great clarity. It has been a privilege to get to know each man through his writings.

I am especially indebted to the works of Fred Kelly, Tom Crouch and Fred Howard. Kelly's real-life collaboration with Orville resulted in the publication of *The Wright Brothers,* the only authorized biography of them; the first collection of their letters, *Miracle at Kitty Hawk;* and Orville's court deposition, *How we Invented the Airplane,* which Kelly edited. Crouch provides masterful background information and interpretation of the Wrights' motivations. Fred Howard has written technical explanations of the Wrights' work, so a layperson can understand the significance of the Wrights' achievement.

The actual papers and writings of the Wright brothers have provided wonderful primary source material. The two-volume set, *The Papers of Wilbur and Orville Wright,* collected and edited by Marvin W. McFarland, and *The Published Writings of Wilbur and Orville Wright,* edited by Peter L. Jakab and Rick Young, have been invaluable in reconstructing the lives of these two men.

No life is lived in isolation, but is a reflection of a great multitude of influences. At times, those very forces push an individual in a direction quite different from what was intended. The Wrights made choices, some of which ran contrary to firmly held popular beliefs of the time. One of those choices was the belief that man could fly. At the time, few people thought that human flight was possible. By the time they entered the field, several of those who tried to master flight had lost their life trying.

They were inspired by the work of one researcher who tried and paid with his life, Otto Lilienthal. After reading about his work, they became infected with an idea that human flight was possible. That idea was to consume their lives. Once it took hold, they were forever changed. What had once been two very ordinary lives became extraordinary, as they pursued together the solution that had evaded other men for centuries.

Theirs is the story of determination, insight, struggle, success and failure. It is a story worth repeating because, in this world of instant information and excessive gratification, it is essential to periodically refocus on our own impossible dreams and set new goals to ensure that we not lose sight of what we might achieve if only we persist.

It is my sincere hope that those reading this book might find within these pages the inspiration to pursue their "impossible" dreams. The world today desperately needs problem-solvers like the two brothers from Dayton, Ohio, who forever changed our world.

ACKNOWLEDGEMENTS

My dear friend, Reverend Richard Batzler, often speaks of an attitude of gratitude. There are many persons to whom I owe an attitude of gratitude, for their gracious help during the preparation of this book. If I should omit someone, I want to apologize to him or her right now.

The mayor of Kitty Hawk, Bill Harris, was most generous in sharing with me what Kitty Hawk was like at the turn of the century and suggesting several important sources of information. Bill is the grandson of Elijah Baum, the young boy who escorted Wilbur to Captain Tate's home. Bill spent 37 years in the Park Service and was responsible for many of the first flight celebratio ns during the course of his tenure.

Darrell Collins, the historian at the National Wright Memorial, read the manuscript and corrected several inaccurate figures, which I had gleaned from other sources of information. Darrell also wrote the foreword to thi s book. As a historian, Darrell favors these two Wright brothers' quotes. In his first letter to Octave Chanute, Wilbur wrote, "For some years I have been afflicted with the belief that flight is possible to man." In 1929, Orville wrote, " Aviation has gon e beyond my dreams."

Patricia Click, professor of history at the University of Virginia, assisted with the mechanics of writing and offered several suggestions for the presentation of information.

My good friend, Gloria Wingenroth, volunteered to read th e manuscript for errors. Her eagle eye spotted several, which were promptly removed. Her response to the manuscript was most encouraging.

Brandon Edwards was my young adult consultant. Brandon's enthusiasm while reading the manuscript helped me determine that the book was appropriate for the senior high school student, as well as the general adult population.

Ann Woerle, librarian at First Flight Middle School, read the manuscript and offered helpful comments.

Last, but certainly not least, is my husband, Jack Dempsey. To him I owe not only my deepest gratitude, but also a caramel cake. Jack spent many, many hours going through the manuscript looking for mechanical errors and misspellings as well as content. Jack photographed the Wright memorial for the front and back covers and is responsible for the design of the front cover. Without his patience and concentration, this book would never have become a reality.

I am also in debt to the staffs of the Dare County libraries, the Outer Banks History Center, the Island Bookstore in Duck, the National Wright Memorial and Wright State University in Ohio, for their help with ordering materials and pictures during my research.

CHAPTER ONE

THE HOMECOMING

On December 17, 1903, Wilbur and Orville Wright became the first persons in human history to successfully fly a powered, heavier-than-air plane. The 1903 Wright Flyer was the first important invention of the twentieth century, yet it was denied the honor it so richly deserved in the United States and, in 1928, was sent to England to be exhibited at the Science Museum in London. Finally, in 1948, it returned to enjoy a long overdue homecoming at the Smithsonian Institution.

The 1903 Wright Flyer is a visible reminder of the courage, creativity and commitment of aviation's most famous pioneers, Orville and Wilbur Wright. Their work was an important step in the advancement of aeronautical science that has reached its present peak in space travel. Without it, we might still be without another first, a photograph of our earth "in all its spherical glory." On December 7, 1972 the crew of Apollo 17 captured our planet in a photograph entitled *The Blue Marble,* which has become NASA's most popular photograph. Apollo 17's monumental feat is a culmination of decades of technological advances, all of which built on the Flyer's proof that man can, indeed, fly.

Apollo 11 landed on the moon in July 1969 and Neil Armstrong became the first man to set foot on its surface, the words he spoke that day are remembered today and often repeated, "That's one small step for a man . . . one giant leap for mankind."

Less known and seldom repeated are the words telegraphed to Bishop Wright by his two sons as they attempted their first powered flight on December 14, 1903, "Success assured. . . ." Three days later success became reality, as Orville Wright flew 120 feet in twelve seconds from level ground in a heavier-than-air, powered machine for the first time in human history.

Captain Louis F. Ferber, one of the earliest French aviators, begrudgingly conceded that the Wrights were the first to conquer the air. He admitted that the Wrights had done everything in the air first. He is reported to have said that no matter how one tries to explain the facts away, the truth remains, the Wrights were the first to fly. They were the first men who successfully made "powered, sustained, controlled flights."

THE BLUE MARBLE

On November 2, 2000, Yuri Gidzenko, Bill Shepherd and Sergei Krikalev became the first residents of the International Station encircling the earth.

In November 2002, a tiny band of Nature Conservancy volunteers stood on the same sandy, wind-swept shore that the Wright brothers had and cheered as the Space Shuttle, *Endeavor,* zoomed past and out of sight. It had been launched eight minutes earlier at Cape Kennedy.

One hundred years after the Wright brothers' first flight we are still awed by our ability to fly and we continue to extend our reach farther and farther into space. But if it hadn't been for the tenacity and commitment of Orville and Wilbur Wright a century ago, space flight would not be as advanced today. The world has never been the same since that fateful day when Orville Wright first flew.

Due to some unfortunate circumstances, the relationship between the Wrights and the Smithsonian Institution became strained and in 1928 Orville Wright sent the Wright Flyer to England where it remained for the next twenty years.

The 1903 Flyer had survived the German blitz over London where it had been stored underground, but it almost didn't survive the New York dock strike. The director of the British Science Museum accompanied the 1903 Flyer when it crossed the Atlantic aboard the ocean liner, *Mauritania*. But when Paul E. Garber, Historian Emeritus of the National

Air and Space Museum, arrived at the New York Customs House to claim the Flyer, he found that the captain of the *Mauritania* had learned of the strike and had decided to unload the Flyer at Halifax, Nova Scotia. Garber then made arrangements for the Flyer to be transported by the escort carrier, *U.S.S. Palau.*

When the Navy carrier finally docked at Bayonne, New Jersey, a crew from the Smithsonian was waiting with a large Navy truck bearing the label, **"Operation Homecoming."** Garber wrote that the journey to Washington was more like a "triumphal procession" with police escorts at most towns and a stop at the Wright Aeronautical Corporation so the employees could pay their respects to the first successful powered plane.

RECONSTRUCTION OF 1903 WRIGHT FLYER

A Smithsonian reception committee met the crated Flyer at the Freer Gallery of Art. After the ceremony, the boxes were moved to the Arts and Industries Building. The Flyer was home, but much work still had to be done to prepare it for exhibit.

Garber and the members of The Early Birds of Aviation, men who had worked on and flown the earliest Wright airplanes, reconstructed the Flyer and removed any signs of deterioration. The Wright Flyer joined other pioneer flyers, the Wright 1909 Military Flyer and the *Vin Fizz.* Charles Lindbergh said that one of the highest honors given to the Spirit of St. Louis was being exhibited in the same hall as the Wright Flyer.

RECONSTRUCTION OF 1903 WRIGHT FLYER

On December 17, 1948, nearly a year after Orville Wright passed away, his nephew, Milton Wright, formally presented the reconstructed 1903 Wright Flyer to the Smithsonian Institution. It was the forty-fifth anniversary of the first heavier-than-air, manned, powered flight. In his remarks Milton Wright said:

> The world has come to think of Orville and Wilbur Wright either as demigods whose minds suddenly produced the answer to the problem of flight or as ignorant mechanics, who stumbled on the secrets of flight. They were neither. They were normal young men who had an idea and saw a problem and set about to solve that problem. Their ability to select the vital parts of their problem and to discard the unessential was an important factor in their success.

> It was a happy combination of circumstances that, through the seemingly commonplace beginnings, the years of painstaking work to perfect the plane, and later to gain recognition for it, neither of the brothers ever abandoned the vision of this first plane as the symbol of the turning point; the concrete evidence that what was impossible before is now universally accepted practice (Young, 182, 184).

No one today doubts that a manned, heavier-than-air, powered machine can fly, but that was not always true. In fact, it is only within the last century that man has been able to fly. Before then, men who thought flight was possible were considered fools and dreamers, not visionaries.

But the Wrights were truly visionaries, inspired by the work of other aeronautical visionaries like Cayley, Lilienthal and Chanute. Before the Wrights began their work, they studied the works of those visionaries and then proceeded to develop their own vision. They used what they found to be true and discarded the "facts" which were in conflict with what they had experienced. What wasn't known, they set out to find through extensive experiments.

Even in the face of apparent failure and at times intense self-pity, they persisted, and then proceeded to verify and clarify their hunches with numerous tests and endless discussions until their concepts were refined to the point of possibility.

At that point, they demonstrated the impossible; they flew. They accomplished what man from the beginning of time had hoped to do. The difference between the Wrights and all other dreamers was that they made their dream a reality.

But it was not without great cost. They endured financial, physical and emotional loss. In 1908, Orville was seriously injured at the first U.S. Army demonstrations and suffered from severe pain for the rest of his life. Two of the brothers' closest friends turned on them. Wilbur was so drained by the strain of preparing for patent infringement suits and testifying in court that he had no resistance to the progression of typhoid fever that took his young life. Eventually, Orville withdrew from public life, maintaining only those contacts most important to the future of flight, the preservation of the 1903 Wright Flyer and honoring the memory of his brother.

But theirs is a glorious story, which should inspire others to follow their own dreams and use their special talents and skills to improve their world.

CHAPTER TWO

THE WRIGHT STUFF

In the latter half of the nineteenth century, the Wright family was living in Cedar Rapids, Iowa. Milton Wright, Orville and Wilbur's father, was a minister who traveled frequently on church business. During his many long absences, his wife, Susan, was responsible for managing their five active youngsters - four boys, and a girl. This was no easy task for a woman at that time, but Susan Wright had an extraordinary gift for nurturing each of her children's unique talents. At the time, she had no idea that one day their two youngest sons, Orville and Wilbur, would solve the problem of human flight and give to the people of the world the ability to fly on man-made wings. That day would not come for many years, but Susan's part in giving this gift to the world was the patient encouragement of her children.

Even as an eight-year-old child, Orville Wright was extremely curious. He always wanted to know what would happen if he tried to do this or that. One day he tried to discover what would occur if he filled an old oil-can with water and set it on the wood-burning stove. He didn't have long to wait. Within minutes, the over-heated water squirted out of the nozzle a foot into the air.

Fred Howard reports in his book, *Wilbur and Orville,* that Orville was so impressed by the result of his experiment that on April 1, 1881, he wrote his father about it. His son's letter must have delighted Milton Wright, who was traveling at the time.

Dear Father,

I got my letter today. My teacher said I was a good boy. We have 45 in our room. The other day I took a machine can and filled it with water then I put it on the stove. I waited a little while and the water came squirting out of top about a foot. [. . .] The old cat is dead (5).

There is no hint of remorse for the mess he must have created or any indication that he was ever scolded for putting that can of water on the stove. In fact, he seems to have taken pride in his discovery that the steam from boiling water can produce a powerful thrust of energy. This concept of thrust remained dormant until many years later when he and Wilbur were experimenting with flying machines.

Whatever Orville's fascination with cause and effect, it was nurtured by his mother, Susan Catherine Koerner Wright. She possessed a talent for fixing things, even making her own appliances. She inherited this mechanical aptitude from her father, a carriage-maker, who owned a fine piece of Indiana bottomland where he conducted a thriving carriage business.

When Orville visited the farm, he was especially impressed with Grandfather Koerner's carriage shop, which had a large foot-driven lathe. Years later, Orville persuaded his mother to help him make just such a lathe. It was not unusual for any of the Wright children to ask their mother for mechanical advice. When the two older sons, Reuchlin and Lorin, longed for a sled, it was she who designed and constructed it. Long after her death, the boys still spoke about that cherished sled.

It is no surprise that Susan Wright was tolerant of her sons' tinkering. It was this talent that initiated the first frail steps toward what would become, many decades later, the first "small step for man" as Neil Armstrong stepped onto the surface of the moon in 1969.

As Susan Koerner Wright nurtured her sons' problem-solving skills, she never could have imagined how their mechanical ability and their capability to visualize complex solutions would lead them to develop a machine man could fly.

Milton Wright encouraged his children to think, the same as his older brothers had urged him. As a former teacher, he deplored the word-guessing method of reading being taught in the schools, so he taught his own children to read and write before they entered public school.

Milton Wright had been born to homesteaders in east-central Indiana. It was frontier country, complete with bears, wolves and trappers wandering the woods. Life there was hard. Society was harder. Disagreements were settled with violence. Dan Wright, Milton's father, built the family cabin, cleared the land and planted corn, all by hand. His mother, Catherine, ground the corn, made the clothes and bore the children.

When Milton was twelve years old, the family moved. It was then that Milton discovered books. He read whenever his chores were done and practiced public speaking while he worked in the fields. At fifteen, he experienced a religious conversion. He later reported there was no immediate revelation but rather a quiet peace and joy, unlike any he had ever experienced before. Milton Wright remained a committed Christian for the rest of his life.

He studied doctrine for five years before he decided to join the Church of the United Brethren of Christ and was baptized. In 1841, the church constitution supported a personal relationship with God and the election of bishops by delegates to the General Conference. Members were to abstain from alcohol and urged to support the anti-slavery cause. Membership in secret societies was forbidden. In 1853, Milton was admitted to the White River Conference, the local church governing body. That same year he was appointed supervisor of the Hartsville College preparatory department and took college courses there but never graduated.

It was unusual for a woman in the 1850s to be educated beyond high school, but Susan's father wanted her to receive a college education, so he sent her to Hartsville College. It was there that she and Milton met. Milton Wright appreciated Susan Koerner's ability to think and found her shyness attractive.

He was ordained a minister of the United Brother Church of Christ in August 1856. He accepted a mission call to the Oregon Territory a year later. He proposed to Susan, but she wished to wait until after his three-year commitment, and, if they were both still willing, they could be married. When he returned to Indiana, they were married. It was Thanksgiving Day, November 22, 1859.

Susan was all that Milton had wished for in a wife. With his many absences for church business, the responsibilities of managing the children and home fell to her. Whatever education and skill she possessed, she channeled into her life as wife and mother. It is to her credit that her children flourished in spite of many moves and the many absences of Reverend Wright.

It is in this stimulating environment that Orville and Wilbur Wright were reared. Orville said in an interview for Fred Kelly's biography, *The Wright Brothers*:

> [We] *did* have special advantages [. . . .] [It was] simply that we were lucky enough to grow up in a home environment where there was always much encouragement to children to pursue intellectual interests; to investigate whatever aroused curiosity. In a different kind of environment our curiosity might have been nipped long before it could have borne fruit (28).

CHAPTER THREE

A CHILDHOOD REMEMBERED

Although Milton Wright traveled as far away as the West Coast, his young family was never far from his mind. He frequently wrote his children interesting letters about his adventures, attempting to stimulate their imaginations in his absence. Milton wrote about the Dakota and Montana territories where he met Flathead and Blackfeet Indians, whom he said were quite friendly.

As a former educator, Milton was well aware that his growing children required a point of reference in order to understand what he was writing, so he often offered comparisons, such as the size of the town of Missoula compared to a town the children knew, Dublin, Indiana.

He must have enthralled his young family with his description of his harrowing train ride over the mountains. He stated that those mountains had some of the steepest grades he had ever seen trains travel across. One was so steep that two locomotives were needed, one to pull and one to push the train around the horseshoe bends and down the other side.

After attending a fair on the West Coast, he wrote that he had seen two pumpkins that were as big as boulders and pomegranates the size of apples.

Milton surely captured the children's vivid imaginations when he wrote about a sea serpent, which was spotted in the waters off the California coast. He described it as being 60-120 feet long with a bright crest on its head. He stated that it performed like a whale and sounded like a dying horse. However, Milton conceded it was probably a fish story and promised to go see for himself.

BISHOP MILTON WRIGHT

Milton and Susan used the funds they had acquired from wedding gifts to purchase a five-acre farm in Millville, Indiana. That is where their third son, Wilbur, was born on April 16, 1867. Milton said that at fifteen months of age, Wilbur went into a room, saw everything he could get in to and got into the greatest mischief first.

Milton was appointed professor of theology at Hartsville College, which meant the family needed to move. This would be one of many moves the young family made to accommodate Milton's rising status in the ministry.

Signs of disagreement over the church's anti-Mason policy became apparent at its General Conference in 1869. Milton Wright was firmly committed to equal opportunity for all men and women regardless of race. He detested the fact that Masons gave preference to its members in business and politics. He would spend much of his life fighting to keep this section of the church's constitution. Eventually the conflict led to a split in the church.

At the conference, Milton was elected editor of the church paper, *The Religious Telescope,* which was published in Dayton, Ohio. In June of 1869, Susan, Milton and their three young sons - Reuchlin, Lorin, and Wilbur- moved to Dayton. Shortly after their arrival, Susan delivered twins who died a short time later. The following year Milton purchased a house on Hawthorne Street which became the Wright family residence from 1871 to 1879 and then again from 1885 to 1914.

Many memories were created in that house. One of the first was the birth of Orville Wright on August 19, 1871. Katharine Wright was born exactly three years later. The brother and sister would become allies for life. Orville was Katharine's defender, seeing to it that she was included in all the children's games. Many years later, Katharine nursed Orville through typhoid fever and a serious flying accident. When Wilbur and Orville were in Kitty Hawk experimenting with their flying machines, Orville wrote lengthy, humorous letters to Katharine describing their progress.

A mechanical toy his father purchased for his fifth birthday fascinated Orville. It was a gyroscope, which balanced on the blade of a knife. This top made such a lasting impression on Orville that decades later he told his biographer, Fred Kelly, about it.

Orville found kindergarten far less exciting than playing with his friend, Ed Sines. He obediently left home each morning for school then stopped two doors down where he and Ed spent the day playing. He returned home each day right on time, managing to fool his mother for an entire month. The hoax was discovered the day his mother visited the school, only to learn he had not returned after the first few days. From then on his attendance was quite regular.

Orville's entrepreneurial skills became apparent at a young age. In an effort to support his growing hobbies, he and his friend collected old bones from yards, alleys and vacant lots. For this enormous expenditure of energy they earned a grand total of three cents.

In 1878 Milton was elected bishop and the family moved to Cedar Rapids, Iowa. One day he returned from his travels bearing a unique gift for his two youngest sons. It was a toy helicopter made of paper, cork and bamboo. When the rubber band which powered it was released, the helicopter soared high into the air. The deep impression made by this toy helicopter was the beginning of their interest in flying and is mentioned several times in their writings.

Wilbur made a larger version of the model and tried to fly it. Unfortunately, the larger model was a great disappointment. Years later would he discover why it was such a failure.

Orville was such an excellent student he got promoted to the third grade by reading his second-grade reader while holding it upside down. The principal decided any student who had memorized the book was smart enough to be promoted before the end of the year.

When the family moved to Richmond, Indiana, Orville went into the kite-making business. He was so skillful at making and flying his own kite that all his new friends wanted ones just like his.

The first joint project of Wilbur and Orville was constructing a seven-foot treadle-driven lathe. Wilbur sought to improve the lathe's performance by installing clay ball bearings but the barn shook so much when they ran the large lathe that Orville ran from the building. Once outside he discovered that Katharine was pressed flat against the side of the barn. It was then he realized that it was not the machine that had shaken the barn, but a small cyclone passing through the area.

Wilbur was fascinated with reading and read many different subjects. This gave him not only a vast fund of knowledge but also an excellent grasp of words and their power. Wilbur demonstrated that he was an effective writer when he became the publicity chairman for a circus that Orville and his friends organized.

Orville had discovered that the Johnston's barn was a treasure trove of mounted animal specimens from Mr. Johnston's practice of taxidermy. There were numerous birds and two very large bears - a black bear and a grizzly. What could be better than to have a circus with a bunch of stuffed animals? At least that's what Orville thought. A great group organizer, Orville enlisted the help of Gansey Johnston and Harry Morrow. Thus the circus became The Great W. J. & M. Circus.

As sixteen year-old Wilbur watched this flurry of activity, he inquired whether anyone had thought to inform the press of the unique presentation being planned. Of course, no one had. Wilbur volunteered. His use of words like "mammoth," "colossal" and "menagerie" was so convincing that the publicity article was published in the daily *Item.*

The day of the circus parade, nine-year-old "Corky" Johnston, who was to be Davy Crockett, got into an argument with his brother, Gansey, and was banished from the parade by the "circus bosses." His brother, five-year-old Griswold, was then drafted to take his place as Davy Crockett. Although his father's hunting clothes were several sizes too big for him, he would just have to do. Another partner, Harry Morrow, had to go to Michigan with his family. In spite of all these minor inconveniences, the advance publicity was so successful that hordes of people lined the parade route.

The first performance was so packed, a second performance was scheduled. A disgruntled Corky Johnston announced there would be no second performance. Earlier Orville had presented a circus with another friend. It had featured the boy's Shetland pony and was such a great hit that Mr. Miller, the boy's father, gave the staff and spectators a lavish reception with ice cream, cake and lemonade. Everyone said that the day was a great success.

Milton and Susan must have wondered what their industrious sons would do next.

CHAPTER FOUR

RETURN TO DAYTON

In 1885, Susan Wright was packing once again. She must have wondered how many more times she would assemble all their possessions and pack them into barrels and boxes so the family could move. She no longer had the stamina of her younger days. In those days moving didn't seem to be such a problem.

Gathering all the kitchen utensils and clothes and the vast variety of family treasures was such a physical strain. She had to pack them so carefully that they would arrive at their new destination without being broken. She knew if the porcelain doll Orville had given Katharine were broken, both children would be upset.

The two older boys, Reuchlin and Lorin, had left Hartsville College after a year of study and were living in Dayton. Susan was relieved that they were in Dayton because they could set up the rented house before she and Katharine arrived. She must have wished the family were going to their own house on Hawthorne Street, but that was being rented. It would be four months before they could move back there.

When Orville arrived home from sixth grade and announced that he was unable to return to school until a parent visited the school, it was almost too much for her to handle. Orville was a good boy but always getting into some kind of trouble. Milton had already made arrangements for shipping all their belongings by train. She just couldn't take the time to visit a school Orville wouldn't be attending in the fall.

There is no evidence that Susan Wright ever questioned her husband's deep religious convictions or that she resented the emotional impact his devotion to the early church constitution had on their family. All indications are that Susan supported her zealous husband in his quest to uphold the prohibition of Masonic membership. It may in fact have been Susan's loyal support for Milton that later led Wilbur to work in defense of his father's cause.

During the years that the Wrights lived in Richmond, Indiana, many seeds of interest were sown. These eventually became full-grown when Orville and Wilbur reached maturity.

At age twelve, Orville was intrigued with the prints from woodcuts he found in the *Century* magazine. Once his curiosity was aroused, he started reading everything he could find about how to make them and was soon engraving woodcuts of his own. The source of his material was the family woodpile. His pocketknife and its spring became his engraving tools. Milton's letterpress made a handy printing press for his new creations.

Susan took as much pride in her youngest son's achievements as she did Wilbur's scholarly pursuits and his photographic memory. She must have breathed a sigh of relief that Wilbur and Orville's frequent friction was finally lessening. They had collaborated so well on the circus presentation that the community was greatly impressed by them.

The move back to Dayton was to be a positive one. They became reacquainted with old friends and returned to the Hawthorne house, which they all enjoyed. Just as soon as they were settled back on Hawthorne Street, Orville went to see his young friend, Ed Sines. Imagine his surprise and delight when he discovered that Ed, too, was interested in printing. In fact, Ed owned a miniature printing set. The two friends then proceeded to set up shop in Mrs. Sines' kitchen.

HAWTHORNE STREET HOUSE

Fred Kelly reported in his biography that when an envelope addressed to "Messrs. Sines & Wright" arrived, Mrs. Sines commented, "It must be you for you certainly are a pair of messers" (30).

13

Milton was intrigued by his youngest son's new interest and persuaded the two older boys, Lorin and Wilbur, to donate their unused press to their enthusiastic sibling. He then purchased the twenty-five pounds of brevier type that put the amateur printers in business.

Orville and Ed Sines set up their new press in larger quarters, the Wrights' barn. Those spacious surroundings only added to their enthusiasm and the two boys became the firm of "Sines and Wright". Since a printer needs to print, they proceeded to compose, publish and distribute a three-page newspaper, the *Midget,* for the benefit of their fellow eighth graders. All went well until Milton happened on a copy and turned to the third page. This consisted of the words "Sines and Wright" in large, bold type printed diagonally across the entire page.

Perhaps it was the lack of initiative or maybe it was the promise to print in the following issue one of Miss Jenning's famous lectures before the pupils of the intermediate school on the "Inherent Wickedness of School Children," but whichever it was, Bishop Milton Wright banned the publication of the *Midget.*

In Richmond, Wilbur had completed all his course requirements to graduate high school but he never received his diploma. He had his sights set on going to Yale, but since he needed additional courses to pass the entrance exam, he enrolled at Central High in Dayton in the fall of 1884. He took courses in science, trigonometry and history. Those courses became the well of knowledge from which he drew later, when he and Orville began their quest for manned flight.

Wilbur was agile in both mind and body. He played on the football team and in several other sports. In the winter of 1885, while playing ice hockey, he collided with an opponent's hockey stick. It struck his jaw with such force that it knocked out his front teeth. A surgeon from the Soldier's Home, where they were playing, dressed the wound and offered to escort Wilbur home. Wilbur declined the offer and walked home, worried that his mother would be frightened if she saw someone bringing him home.

Life changed dramatically for Wilbur. He underwent painful dental work and lived on a restricted diet of eggs, toast and tea. He experienced heart palpitations and nausea. A lengthy period of convalescence was prescribed. The psychological impact was devastating. Instead of seeing himself as a confident student and an excellent athlete, he began to think of himself as frail and vulnerable.

As the convalescence lengthened, Wilbur became increasingly depressed. All hope of a college degree seemed to have vanished. His losses were enormous; his budding friendship with a fellow female student faltered; prospects for a professional life dimmed; his peer relationships suffered; and participation in contact sports became impossible. Now the Wright family had two invalids, for Susan had been diagnosed with tuberculosis and her illness was progressing rapidly. She needed constant care. As Wilbur's physical wounds healed, he assumed responsibility for the care of his mother. Not only did he prepare her meals and carry her up and down the steps, but also he made her a wooden rocking chair.

When Milton spoke of his son's devotion to his mother, he said that Wilbur had given of himself with such tenderness that, when it was Wilbur's turn to die, he should be consoled by the memory of these actions of service to his mother.

Milton felt that his wife had not been in pain, but had declined slowly due to effects of her illness. He credited the care Susan received from Wilbur with extending Susan's life by at least two years.

Through Milton's testimony we learn that Wilbur was attentive to the needs of his mother. But, Susan was probably just as attentive to Wilbur's needs. This was a woman who had devoted her whole life to nurturing her family. Surely, no one was more acutely aware of Wilbur's depression than Susan. It must have grieved her greatly to see her promising son caught in the web of hopeless depression. It may have been Susan who urged Wilbur to begin reading. Their home was a reservoir of intellectual materials. Perhaps she asked him to read to her from the works of Hawthorne, Sir Walter Scott or another classic.

Soon Wilbur was educating himself. He learned about the momentous events of ancient and modern history. He studied ethics and the principles of science. During his latter years of melancholy, he became increasingly active in events outside the home.

The Church of the United Brethren in Christ had appointed a commission to study the growing conflict over membership in secret societies and to propose a new constitution. The commission's sessions were held in secret but, in the fall of 1885, non-commission members were permitted at the final session. Wilbur had availed himself of this opportunity to learn what was being discussed. He took careful notes on all the changes, which were approved, to the traditional Constitution and Confessions of Faith. When the official version of these new documents was made public in January of 1887, Wilbur was appalled at the additional changes that had been made. They differed so drastically from what was approved in that final session that Wilbur wrote a pamphlet entitled *Scenes in the Church Commission*. Three thousand copies of the pamphlet were printed and mailed in 1888. Another eleven hundred were distributed at local conferences and in church congregations.

The pamphlet came to the attention of a liberal church official who expressed consternation at the audacity of a youth who would question issues decided upon by elders of the church. Wilbur responded that the liberals had been dissatisfied because they thought the radicals were out of step with reality and couldn't wait for these "old men" to pass away. Yet, when a younger man had spoken on behalf of the radicals' position they complained and accused that man of not telling the truth. Wilbur asked at what age do men become capable of telling the truth. He wondered if the truth of a person's statement can be determined by the age of that person. He said he knew persons as young as five who had spoken the truth.

This would not be the last time that Wilbur came to the aid of his father's cause. In the coming years Wilbur would defend his father and his position several more times before Milton retired.

Finally, Wilbur's fire was back. It was obvious that he had recovered his self-confidence, had a firm grasp of the language and was fully able to use it to defend his point of view, and was a determined defender of truth in the face of daunting opposition. These traits would become increasingly important to Wilbur as he would need them to defend the Wright patent in future court battles.

HAWTHORNE STREET HOUSE

CHAPTER FIVE

A GREAT LOSS

Not long after Milton had left for the West Coast in August 1888, Wilbur wrote him that Susan had not requested his early return, but she would be comforted by his presence. In all the years of his traveling, Susan had managed to cope without her husband, but as her disease took its toll, she needed him with her.

The emotional impact upon the Wright family of both Susan's illness and the ongoing battle within the Church of the United Brethren in Christ was devastating. Reuchlin had married and was having a rough time making ends meet. Lorin moved away, having decided to seek his fortune in the West. Wilbur was using his pent-up frustrations lobbying on behalf of his father's cause. Katharine was striving to meet Milton's expectations of her as his "nice pet daughter." Only Orville *seemed* to be blossoming as he worked nearly sixty hours a week in a local print shop during the long, hot summer.

A spark seemed to have been ignited in Orville during his sophomore year of high school and his grades improved dramatically. The printing establishment of Sines and Wright was gaining business printing pamphlets, business stationary and cards, and running advertisements for local merchants.

Just when everything seemed to be going very well for the young firm, the boys completed a printing job for $2.00 worth of popcorn still on the cob. Orville verified this estimate of worth with a local grocer. Ed Sines wanted to eat the profits, but Orville wanted to invest the capital in purchasing additional type. When they were unable to reach a compromise, the partnership of Sines and Wright dissolved.

Orville had aspirations of publishing a community newspaper. It would be a simple paper and concentrate mostly on local affairs. He even selected a name, *The West Side News*. What he didn't have was a press large enough to print the paper. Being ever resourceful, he improvised, just as he had done when he used an old gravestone in building the press for the firm of Sines and Wright.

Since he had more ingenuity than money, he hunted for materials, which were readily available to him, like the family woodpile. There he found four-foot lengths of firewood to make the frame. He located pieces of iron and steel in the local junkyard. In the family barn he found an old buggy, which had steel bars to hold the buggy's top open. These bars were just what were needed to apply pressure to the press.

Wilbur took an intense interest in his younger brother's current flurry of activity. After making several pointed suggestions, he offered to help. Soon he was just as involved as Orville. The changes he made to the moving parts of the press were quite unorthodox, but they greatly improved the performance of the machine.

Word of this unusual printing press spread. One day a well-dressed gentleman came into the shop and asked to have a look at it. He removed his coat, lay flat on the floor and examined every aspect of the press. When he had satisfied his curiosity, he got up, put on his coat and stated that it worked all right, but he didn't understand why. As he left, he placed a business card on the table. When Orville looked at the card, he discovered the gentleman was the press foreman from a Denver newspaper.

The first issue of *The West Side News* was published on March 1,1889. In it, Orville stated:

> This week we issue the first number of *The West Side News*, a paper to be published in the interests of the people and business institutions of the West Side. Whatever tends to their advancement, moral, mental and financial, will receive our close attention.

Ed Sines, now an employee, solicited advertisements and some news items. Wilbur began to write humorous essays and future poet, Paul Laurence Dunbar, a school friend of Orville's, contributed poems and other articles of interest. Soon the masthead on *The West Side News* listed Wilbur as the editor and Orville as the publisher.

The General Church Conference was held in York, Pennsylvania, in May 1889. Much to the dismay of the entire Wright family, the elders of the United Brethren Church voted to accept the new constitution and creed. Fifteen of the conference delegates left the conference and set up the Church of the United Brethren in Christ (Old Constitution). Bishop Milton Wright was among them. Crouch wrote that the *Christian Conservator* reported, "When all the other bishops faltered and fell prostrate before the commission compromise with the world, he (Bishop Wright) stood faithful among the faithless, and deserves great credit from every United Brethren" (82).

Just as her youngest sons were reaching maturity and her revered husband had experienced a major defeat, Susan was nearing the end of her life. In her latter years, she had been the hub around which the whole family revolved.

Orville loved to delight his mother with his stories of building the larger press and beginning the weekly newspaper. More than likely, it was Susan who encouraged him in these pursuits. And when Orville became frustrated with finding only four-foot lengths of wood in the family woodpile, Susan most likely suggested he pay a modest price for the longer boards at the lumberyard. She probably was the one who gave Orville permission to disassemble the family buggy top so he could use the iron bars to provide the needed pressure for the new press.

Three months before her death, Orville had begun to publish *The West Side News*. Wilbur joined Orville as editor of the paper. Wilbur enjoyed his role as editor because it allowed him to use his intellectual strengths. This collaboration must have pleased Susan, for now both her youngest sons were doing work they found rewarding.

Fifteen-year-old Katharine was blossoming into a young woman. Susan surely provided the necessary feminine instructions and guidance that young girls require. Katharine undoubtedly had been involved in household tasks from an early age. The womanly responsibilities for managing a household at the turn of the century were very physically demanding, from the scrubbing of clothes and floors, to baking breads and pies, to making clothes and beating rugs.

Susan was pleased when Katharine spoke of going to college and wanting to become a teacher of children. After all, Susan herself had gone to college and wouldn't have wanted less for her own daughter. Katharine excelled in her school and had the social graces that Susan had found so difficult because of her shyness.

Although Milton had experienced the worst defeat of his career in May of 1889, he was resilient and didn't take it lying down. He rallied the old constitution forces and set up the Church of the United Brethren in Christ (Old Constitution). Even though he was physically exhausted, he was mentally stimulated and prepared for the court battles he knew were ahead.

But ravages of tuberculosis had sapped Susan's body. She had given all a wife and mother could give and was ready to pass to her eternal rest knowing that her family would survive without her physical presence. Her freedom came on July 4, 1889. In *Twelve Seconds to the Moon,* Young and Fitzgerald printed Wilbur's tribute to his mother:

> After many years of affliction so heroically borne, our mother has gone from among us. Mrs. Susan Wright, wife of Bishop Milton Wright, died at noon, on the Fourth of July at the family residence on Hawthorne Street in the fifty-ninth year of her life. We children learned to look upon mother as almost perfection itself. No kinder mother ever lived than ours; none loved her children more; none who more unselfishly sacrificed her own comforts and joys to pleasure and happiness to those she loved. For nearly eight years, she has been afflicted with lung disease and has gradually declined in health, but in that time no one ever heard one word of complaint pass her lips. Her clearness of mind, patience and endurance have the more endeared her to her family (12).

Silent tears were shed that day and the day of her burial as her lifeless body was lowered into the grave. Yet even in this sorrow, there was a sense of joy that finally the suffering of their beloved mother was over.

Susan Wright could not have known at her passing that soon a new chapter would open for her industrious sons. Within a matter of a few short years the initiative and inventiveness, which she nurtured would blossom into the passion which fueled their pursuit of manned flight. But that was still a few years away.

CHAPTER SIX

REORIENTATION

As devastating as it was, the death of Susan Wright also marked a new beginning for the Wright family. Her death was surely a grave loss for the older sons, Reuchlin and Lorin, who were no longer living in Dayton. But her absence did not have the same impact on them as it had upon those who had seen her daily. The residents of 7 Hawthorne St. had to reorient themselves to life without the wife and mother who had nurtured and supported them. It must have been a very difficult time, yet each of them had a vast reservoir of positive experiences from which to draw the strength they needed to make the adjustment.

Wilbur enjoyed the challenge of being a newspaper editor. He urged Orville to make the paper a daily. On April 30, 1890, *The Evening Item* began as a daily. It cost one cent a day. From all accounts it was a good community paper. It carried items of national and international interest as well as local news. However, the competition from the papers with high-.speed presses was so stiff the Wrights ran the paper only three months. The last issue was published in August 18, 1890. The Wrights' bread and butter then became job printing, pamphlets, annuals, posters and business stationery.

Every relationship has its kinks to work out. The Wright brothers were no exception Orville had the enthusiasm and initiative to begin the printing and publishing company. Wilbur came on board first as a helper, then as an editor, then as a full partner. This relationship seemed to succeed most of the time but at times Orville still felt he was being treated as the "little brother."

The brothers had agreed to build a press for another firm. After work on it began, they received a contract for an enormous printing job for the Church of the United Brethren in Christ. The brothers decided that Wilbur would build the press and Orville would do the printing and binding for the church contract. Whether it was the tediousness of the printing and binding job or the missed challenge of building the new press that upset Orville is unknown. What is known is that Orville felt he got the worst end of the bargain and wanted to renegotiate.

After much discussion and very little agreement, Wilbur was exasperated. He drew up a mock brief to present to the "Circuit Court of Hawthorne Street."

In his brief, Wilbur requested that the court rule on the appropriate division of the funds received from the completion of both contracts. In addition, he asked that an apology be made by Orville for his demeaning behavior toward Wilbur and that Orville refrain from such rude behavior in the future.

This bit of humor eventually defused the situation and set the tone for their future success as partners in their life-long pursuit of manned flight. Wilbur once confessed that he liked to scrap with Orville because Orville was such a good scrapper.

In later years, Carrie Kayler Grumbach, their housekeeper, reported that after their interest in aviation had begun they argued passionately night after night. It was in this mill of heated discussion that they ground the grist of their differing opinions and insights until the pure elements of truth emerged.

They were more than just business partners. They became the closest of friends, even participating in leisure activities together. When Orville purchased one of the new safety bicycles (both of the wheels were the same size), the Columbia, for $150, the more frugal Wilbur purchased a used Eagle bicycle for $80.

They took to biking as ducks take to water. On weekends they rode into the surrounding countryside. Some of their excursions were quite lengthy. Wilbur wrote to Katharine describing one such adventure while visiting the Indian mounds in Miamisburg twenty-five miles away. "We climbed and we 'clumb' and then we climbed again'."

When Wilbur asked a farmer if they were getting to the top of the world, the farmer replied that Centerville was the highest point in the county. It was dark when they began their return trip and Orville's imagination began playing tricks on him. He thought he saw a horse and wagon in front of him and jammed his brakes so hard that he nearly threw himself over the handlebars. When they arrived at the spot where he thought he had seen the wagon, it turned out to be just a puddle in the road.

The brothers joined the YMCA Wheelman's Club and Orville took up racing. He considered himself quite a "scorcher." Wilbur was his "starter" (giving him a push). Orville won two first place awards and a second-place award.

The population was still limited to transportation by the horse and buggy or the steam-driven train, so the safety bike meant increased freedom and more independence. The census of 1890 reported, "Few articles created by man have created so great a revolution in social conditions" (Crouch 106).

The Wrights excelled at mechanics and it wasn't long before friends were asking them to repair their bikes. Both boys enjoyed the challenge of fixing these machines. Before they knew it, they were considering entering the bicycle business. Milton agreed it was a promising prospect.

However, their plans were delayed because, on November 6, 1892, Wilbur was suddenly stricken with a serious attack of appendicitis. Dr. Spitler, who had been Susan's physician, was summoned. The wise doctor wished to avoid a dangerous appendectomy because of the risk of a postoperative infection, which was still a leading cause of death at the turn of the century. Instead, he prescribed bed rest, a bland diet and the avoidance of cold.

Although Wilbur was still having some pain in mid-December, the brothers were able to open their bicycle shop in a rented storefront in which they both sold and repaired bicycles. At the turn of the century, the average annual income was only about $440.00 and buying a bicycle was a major investment; therefore, the Wrights only sold a good quality bicycle.

In a very short time, the bicycle business became their primary business. They soon decided to build their own bicycles. The Wright brothers wrote the following ad for the *Snap Shots* cycling magazine they published:

For a number of months, Wright Cycle Co., have been making preparations to manufacture bicycles. After more delay than we expected, we are at last ready to announce that we will have several samples out in a week or ten days, and will be ready to fill orders before the middle of next month. The WRIGHT SPECIAL will contain nothing but high-grade material (Fisk and Todd 28).

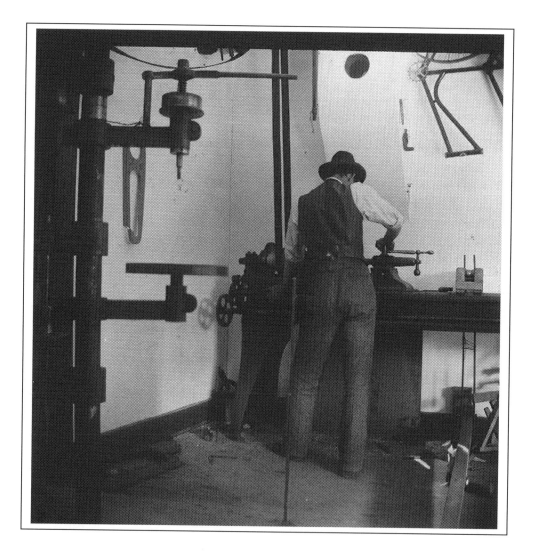

WILBUR WORKING IN THE BICYCLE SHOP

Their top of the line model, the Van Cleve, was named after an ancestor, Catherine *Van* Cleve. A lower-priced model, the St. Clair, received the name of the first governor of the Northwest Territory, Arthur St. Clair.

With Katharine away at Oberlin College and Bishop Wright visiting the western congregations, Orville and Wilbur were often alone in the house. This meant they needed to do their own cooking. Wilbur wrote Katharine assuring her that they were fully capable of surviving on their own:

> We have been living fine. Orville cooks one week and I the next. Orville's week we have bread and butter and meat and gravy and coffee three times a day. My week I give him more variety. You see by the end of the week there is a lot of cold meat stored up, so the first half of my week we have bread and butter and hash and coffee and the last half we have bread and butter and sweet potatoes and coffee (Fitzgerald and Young 14).

As if running two businesses weren't enough, the boys undertook home remodeling projects. To the front of the house they added a wrap-around porch. Inside, they rearranged several rooms and added two gas fireplaces. They planned and executed all this reconstruction themselves. With all their activities, they still found time to read. Wilbur discovered an article in *McClure's Magazine* that piqued his interest. He learned about a German engineer, Otto Lilienthal, who started experimenting with gliders after he had studied the flight of very large birds. Lilienthal was convinced that it was the curve of the bird's wing that enabled it to fly.

When Wilbur shared this article with Orville, the two began lengthy discussions about gliders, birds and flying. Thus the seed, which was planted so many years ago with their father's gift of a toy helicopter, began germinating. It would soon spout and within a very few years become a full-grown interest in human flight.

CHAPTER SEVEN

A GEM OF AN IDEA

If ever the Wrights had a hero, it was the German engineer, Otto Lilienthal. Ever since they had learned about his daring gliding exploits in the "The Flying Man," an article in the September, 1894, issue of *McClure's Magazine,* they had tried to read more about his work.

Lilienthal had become fascinated by the flight of birds in his childhood, but it wasn't until 1879 that he began a serious study of aeronautics. He published the results of his laboratory experiments in the book, *Bird Flight as the Basis of Aviation,* which was written in German.

Lilientha wasn't satisfied with just doing laboratory research; he wanted to fly himself and developed sixteen different types of gliders for manned flight. Some gliders were monoplanes with rear stabilizers, others were biplanes, and several were bat-like structures.

An American reporter, Robert Wood, witnessed several of Lilienthal's courageous flights. He wrote that he had never been as excited or filled with admiration as he was when he watched Otto Lilienthal glide fearlessly through the air.

The young reporter was so enthralled by what he saw that he begged Lilienthal to let him glide. It was then he discovered that balancing the glider was extremely difficult, but he reported that once in the air he felt as if gravity itself had been suspended.

The following day when the glider Lillienthal was flying stalled, he plunged fifty feet to the ground below. He died the next day from a broken neck.

The Wrights were impressed by Lillienthal's work and years later Orville told Fred Kelly that " by his experiments [he] had made more advance in the flying art than had anyone else up to that time." They never changed that opinion (Kelly 47).

Lilienthal's death occurred sometime in August of 1896. That same month Orville was stricken with typhoid fever. The disease was possibly contracted from tainted water and was very prevalent at the turn of the century. Orville suffered severely with high fevers and delirium. His physician, Dr. Spitler, believed the disease would have to run its course. There was little that could be done and no guarantee that Orville would survive.

Katharine was scheduled to begin her fall semester at Oberlin College, but she postponed her return and remained at home to nurse her brother. Wilbur tended the bicycle shop and relieved Katharine as often as he could. Between the older brother and younger sister, Orville received the tenderest of care. He was cooled by ice and fans, given broth and milk to sip and was read to by the hour as he fought for his life.

On October 8, 1896, Bishop Wright noted in his diary, "Orville had tapioca today for the first time. [. . .] He also sat up in bed for the first time in six weeks" (Young and Fitzgerald 16).

The danger was over but Orville still had to regain his strength. When Wilbur felt his brother had sufficiently recovered, he told Orville of Lilienthal's death. In his 1920 deposition, Orville reported that the news of Lilienthal's death increased their interest in the problem of flight and they began looking for books pertaining to the subject ("Invented" 18).

Wilbur dated their renewed interest from the death of Lilienthal:

My own active interest in aeronautical problems dates from back to the death of Lilienthal in 1896. The brief notice of his death, which appeared in the telegraphic news at the time aroused a passionate interest which had existed from my childhood, and led me to take down from the shelves of our home library a book on *Animal Mechanism* by Prof. Marey, which I had read several times (Papers 1: 103).

Still it was not until 1899 that their interest in flying was revived with a reading of James Bell Pettigrew's book, *Animal Locomotion, or Walking, Swimming and Flying, With a Dissertation on Aeronautics*. It was only then that they seriously began to consider the problem of flight. Orville stated:

We could not understand that there was anything about a bird that would enable it to fly that could not be built on a larger scale and used by man.

[. . .] If a bird's wings would sustain it in the air without use of any muscular effort, we did not see why man could not be sustained by the same means ("Invented" 19).

Wilbur also described their thinking at this time.

When a man said, "It can't be done; a man might as well try to fly," he was expressing the final limit of impossibility. Our own growing belief that man might nevertheless learn to fly was based on the idea that, while thousands of the most dissimilar body structures, such as insects, fish, reptiles, birds and mammals, were flying every day at pleasure, it was reasonable to suppose that man might also fly [. . .] (Crouch 161).

The formulation of this belief led Wilbur to write the Smithsonian for additional information. He wanted to avail himself "of all that is already known and then if possible add [his] mite to help on the future worker who will attain final success" (Papers 1: 5)

From this letter it seems apparent that neither Orville nor Wilbur ever thought they would be the ones to eventually solve the major problems of flight.

When Orville saw the letter he became upset because it was written in the first person singular, "I". He complained to Wilbur about this and demanded that all future letters regarding their mutual interest be written in the first person plural, "we". Once again, the older brother syndrome had occurred, but this time it was short lived. The Wright brothers were an extraordinary team, each contributing his unique insights and skills to their joint search for the solution to the problem of flight. Their interest became a shared quest for knowledge. They were well aware that they needed to learn what was already known about flight before they began their own experiments.

When Richard Rathbun, the assistant director of the Smithsonian, replied to Wilbur 's letter, he enclosed several pamphlets: *On Soaring Flight* by E.C. Huffaker; *The Problem of Flying and Practical Experiments in Soaring* by Otto Lilienthal; *Story of Experiments in Mechanical Flight* by Samuel P. Langley; and *Empire of Air* by Louis-Pierre Mouilard. He also recommended *The Aeronautical Annual for 1895-1897*, by James Howard Means; *Progress in Flying Machines* by Octave Chanute; *Experiments in Aerodynamics* by Samuel P. Langley.

The Wrights read and reread these books and pamphlets. They discussed, often heatedly, the contents of each. They discovered that while many men had worked on the problems of flight, no one had yet found a solution.

In *How We Invented The Airplane,* Orville lists several of these researchers:

> Among these who had worked on the problem I may mention Leonardo da Vinci, one of the greatest artists and engineers of all time; Sir George Cayley, who was among the first of the inventors of the internal-combustion engine; Sir Hiram Maxim, inventor of the Maxim rapid-fire gun; Parsons, the inventor of the turbine steam engine; Alexander Graham Bell, inventor of the telephone; Horatio Phillips, a well-known English engineer; Otto Lilienthal, the inventor of instruments used in navigation and a well-known engineer; Thomas A, Edison; and Dr. S.P. Langley, secretary and head of the Smithsonian Institution. Besides these there were a great number of other men of ability who had worked on the problem (20).

Many men had lost their lives attempting to glide, the latest among them were Perry S. Pilcher, a marine engineer, and Otto Lilienthal. Those deaths should have been enough to dissuade sensible men like the Wright brothers, for they were absenters from alcohol and tobacco and cautious users of tea and coffee. They didn't take part in frivolity of any kind. Yet, when it came to the notion of flying, they seemed to throw caution to the wind. We find some clues in what the brothers later wrote.

Mouillard and Lilienthal, the great missionaries of the flying cause "infected us with their own unquenchable enthusiasm, and transformed idle curiosity into the active zeal of workers.
Mouillard had written:

> If there be a domineering, tyrant thought it is the conception that the problem of flight can be solved by man. When once this idea invades the brain, it possesses it completely. It is then a haunting thought, a walking nightmare, impossible to cast off (Young and Fitzgerald 17).

It was too late: the Wrights had already caught the fever. It proved to be an infection, which permeated the rest of their lives. The year was 1899 when they seriously became involved in the quest to solve the problems of flight, which had eluded other men. Wilbur was thirty-two years old and Orville was twenty-eight.

CHAPTER EIGHT

BEGINNINGS

The Wrights were practical men. Some men accumulate knowledge for the pleasure that knowing gives them, while other men learn in order to use the information to make some improvement. The Wrights belonged to the latter group. Although they appreciated knowledge for its own sake, they, like their mother before them, used information to make some needed change. It would have done no good simply to copy what others had done. They had to evaluate what had been accomplished and seek to move beyond the known and leap into the unknown. But how?

Others had extensive training. Horatio Phillips, Otto Lilienthal and Octave Chanute were learned engineers. And Samuel Pierpont Langley was the revered director of the Smithsonian Institution. Yet they failed to master the dynamics that would lead to the ultimate goal, the mastery of the air by manned flight.

In his lecture, "Some Aeronautical Experiments," presented to the Western Society of Engineers on September 18, 1901, Wilbur listed what the brothers had concluded were the basic issues.

The difficulties which obstruct the pathway to success in the flying machine construction are of three general classes: (1) Those that relate to the construction of the sustaining wings; (2) those which relate to the generation and application of the power required to drive the machine through the air; (3) those relating to the balancing of the machine after it is actually in flight (Jakab and Young, 114).

Although the Wrights lacked the formal training of the engineers, they already had accumulated a vast reservoir of practical knowledge through their cycling experiences. They were well aware of the need for balance and control of a machine wheeling through the air with nothing more to sustain it upright than a set of tires in contact with the pavement and the power supplied by the cyclist pumping the pedals.

In 1886, James Means wrote in *The Aeronautical Review* article, "Wheeling and Flying," that learning to ride a bicycle and learning to fly were similar, because in learning both, one needs to learn to balance.

It was this intuitive knowledge plus the intellectual understanding acquired through the reading of the aeronautical literature and their own unique ability to process that information that led the Wrights to the conclusion, that the ultimate problem to be solved was that of balance for, "When this one feature has been worked out, the age of flying machines will have arrived" (Jakab and Young, 115).

In order to understand the complexity of the problem facing the Wrights, it is necessary to think of the airplane as a three-dimensional vehicle which rotates in space around three axes. These axes can be thought of as imaginary lines around which the plane moves. Pitch is an imaginary horizontal line drawn through the center of the plane from wingtip to wingtip. Roll is also an imaginary horizontal line, but it extends through the middle of the plane from nose to tail. Yaw is the only vertical imaginary line and it runs through the center of the plane.

Maintaining balance in these three axes was the problem of control that the Wrights sought to master. It was the problem which had eluded the experts. This was the challenge the Wrights accepted as they proceeded down the path they had chosen for themselves. Wilbur said of their beginnings:

> When we studied [. . .] the loss of life and final failure, which had accompanied all attempts to solve the problem of human flight we understood more clearly than before the immensity and the difficulty of the problem we had taken up. But as we studied the story of their troubles and considered how and why they failed, we could not help thinking that many of their troubles might have been overcome by an adoption of more adequate methods. We began to study the birds.

Now even in their leisure activities, the notion of flight was not far from their consciousness. On their cycling excursion to the Pinnacles, they rested by lying on their backs and watching the birds as they soared in the wind. They noticed that as birds approach the wind, they twist their wing tips changing the angle of the wing as it encounters the wind. From these observations they concluded that the angle of the wing must be capable of change. They reasoned that the angles on the ends of the wingtips that face into the wind must each be different. One wingtip needed to be tipped downward while the other wingtip was tipped upward just as a bird twists the outer edges of its wings as it flies into the wind.

They hypothesized: if the right and left sides of the wing could be twisted, one side would have greater lift than the other side and the equilibrium of the machine would be maintained. It was a novel idea, but how to prove it. In his court deposition years later, which was edited by Fred Kelly and published as *How We Invented The Airplane*, Orville explained:

> The first method that occurred to us for maintaining the lateral equilibrium was that of pivoting the wings on the right and left sides on shafts carrying gears at the center of the machine, which, being in mesh, would cause one wing to turn upward in front when the other wing was turned downward. By this method we thought it would be possible to get a greater lift on one side than on the other, so that the shifting of weight would not be necessary for the maintaining of balance. However, we did not see any method of building this device sufficiently strong and at the same time light enough to enable us to use it (22).

Orville had thought of one possible solution, a three-sectional wing with the center third being stationary while the outer two sections would rotate on a shaft. Structurally the glider would have been too weak for flight and too flexible to move, so that idea was abandoned.

As often happens, inspiration comes when one least expects it. It was as close at hand as the cardboard box Wilbur was absent-mindedly twisting as he waited on a customer one night. Why couldn't a glider's wings be twisted just as he was twisting the sides of this box? We have no idea how quickly he hustled the customer out of the store and locked up for the evening or how fast he pedaled home. What we do know is that as soon as he arrived home, he shared his news with Katharine and her friend, Miss Harriet Silliman, and Orville. These lucky three were treated to the first ever demonstration of wing warping.

MISS HARRIET SILLIMAN AND KATHARINE WRIGHT

In Orville's deposition he tells of this famous demonstration.

> Wilbur showed me a method of getting the same results as we had contemplated in our first idea without the structural defects of the original. He demonstrated the method by means of a small pasteboard box, which had [. . .] the opposite ends removed. By holding the top forward corner and the rear lower corner of one end of the box between his thumb and fore-finger and the rear upper corner and the lower forward corner of the other end of the box in the like manner, and by pressing the corners together, the upper and lower surface of the box were given a helicoidal *(spiral)* twist, presenting the top and bottom surfaces of the box at different angles on the right and left sides.
>
> From this it was apparent that the wings of a machine of the Chanute double-deck type, with the fore-and-aft trussing removed, could be warped in like manner so that, in flying, the wings on the right and left sides could be warped so as to present their surfaces to the air at different angles of incidence and thus secure unequal lifts on the two sides [. . .]
> (23).

Although wing warping was conceived quite by accident, it was a monumental breakthrough for aviation. It allowed the operator to turn the plane right by raising the left wing and lowering the right. In order to turn, left he raised the right wing and lowered the left. In this way the operator controlled lateral balance or roll of the airplane. With this discovery the Wrights had solved one of the major problems of flight which had stymied the experts.

The enthusiasm and energy generated by this discovery of achieving lateral balance through warping the wings motivated them to begin work on the building and the testing of their first glider (1900), which employed wing warping.

The brothers wasted no time. They first constructed a model that incorporated their wing warping principle. It was a biplane with a wing span of five feet and a wing depth of thirteen inches. By attaching cords to the forward corners of the upper and lower wings and the ends of the cords to two sticks held by the operator, the operator could control the movement of the machine. If the operator tipped the upper end of the sticks toward the model, the kite would nose up. If the operator tipped the sticks away from the model, the kite dove toward the ground. Pointing the top of one stick towards the kite and the top of the other stick away from the model caused a roll to one side. If this action were reversed, a roll to the opposite side would occur.

Wilbur tested the kite model at Seminary Hill, about a mile from their home. Several young boys who were playing there watched the experiment with shrieks of delight until the kite darted suddenly towards them. Then they threw themselves face down on the grass.

Among the young observers were two brothers, John and Walter Reiniger, who raced to tell Orville their harrowing tale. Orville was manning the bicycle shop, the brothers' primary source of income.

The enthusiasm generated by this success was all they needed. They were now convinced that this system of balance would be just as effective in a manned glider as it was in their super-kite.

CHAPTER NINE

ON THEIR WAY

In his address to the Western Society of Engineers on September 18, 1901, Wilbur compared learning to fly a plane to learning to ride a boisterous horse. He said:

> Now, there are two ways of learning to ride a fractious horse: One is to get on him and learn by actual practice how each motion and trick may be best met; the other is to sit on a fence and watch the beast a while, and then retire to the house and in leisure figure our the best way of overcoming his jumps and kicks. The latter system is the safest, but the former, on the whole, turns out the larger proportion of good riders. It is very much the same in learning to ride a flying machine; if you are looking for perfect safety, you will do well to sit on a fence and watch the birds; but if you really wish to learn, you must mount a machine and become acquainted with its tricks by actual trial" (Papers 1: 100).

The next step, then, was designing a man-carrying glider. Orville explains: "After a little time we decided to experiment with a man-carrying machine embodying the principle of lateral control used in the kite model already flown" ("Invented" 24).

The glider was planned very carefully. It was a biplane with both wings eighteen feet long and five feet wide. It had 200 square feet of wing surface and flew in 18 mile per hour winds.

Wing warping was accomplished by connecting cables to the front and rear edges of the upper and lower wings. The wires ran over pulleys and were attached to a foot control on the lower wing where the pilot lay. By shifting his feet to one side, the pilot could adjust the length of the cables. In this way, he could pull the edge of the wingtip on one side down, allowing the leading edge of the other side to rise up. This twisting of the wings would permit the pilot to steer the machine either to the right or left. In addition to the main wing surfaces, there was a horizontal rudder four feet in front of the wings. The rudder acted as a counterbalance to movement in the center of pressure upon the wings. It also reduced damage to the glider during take-offs and landings.

In earlier gliders, the curve of the wing was figured on the arc of a circle, which made the curvature quite high. The Wrights planned a shallower arc and moved its high point toward the front of the wing. This reduced wind resistance.

Wilbur viewed the flying of a glider as a balancing game. He stated in his speech:

The balancing of a glider or flying machine is very simple in theory. It consists in causing the center of gravity to coincide with the center of pressure. But in actual practice there seems to be an almost boundless incompatibility of temper, which prevents their remaining peaceably together for a single instant, so that the operator, who in this case acts as a peacemaker, often suffers injury to himself attempting to bring them together (Papers 1: 101).

Whatever changes they made to earlier models were very carefully considered. They were well aware of the dangers involved. Each problem they tackled and solved led them one step closer to powered flight. But not every step led them forward. They would have to retrace many steps and rethink their theories many times before forward progress was made.

On May 4, 1900 Wilbur wrote Octave Chanute, a renowned engineer who had written extensively on aeronautics and is credited by Fred C. Kelly as the best historian of man's attempt to fly. Chanute graciously replied. This was the beginning of a ten-year correspondence. Both men benefited enormously from their relationship. Chanute had experimented with gliders but was never very successful with them. Wilbur needed someone to react to his ideas. Chanute was that person. It was he who encouraged the Wrights to continue experimenting when they were so discouraged. In this letter Wilbur inquired about a suitable place to conduct the gliding experiments. Chanute suggested a location with sand for a soft landing, perhaps San Diego, California or South Carolina.

Wilbur needed more precise information; he wrote the U.S. Weather Bureau in Washington, D.C. Willis Moore, bureau chief, sent him the September and October issues of the official *Monthly Weather Review* for 1899.

Wilbur and Orville poured over those issues and vehemently discussed every pro and con of each possible location. In the end, they chose Kitty Hawk, North Carolina, with average fall winds of 13.4 miles per hour. Kitty Hawk was at the time a remote fishing village located on a barrier island between the Albemarle Sound and the Atlantic Ocean. The entire barrier island is known as the Outer Banks.

Wilbur wrote the Kitty Hawk Weather Bureau for more information on August 3, 1900. His reply came from Joseph J. Dosher, sole staff member of the station. He stated that the beach was a mile wide and free of trees. And the wind at that time of year was from the north and northeast. But there was one small problem: there was no available housing. They would have to camp out.

The Wrights were no strangers to camping out. They often did so with groups of friends. What the brothers didn't understand was the power of nor'easter winds sweeping across the sand dunes and the effect the winds would have upon a canvas structure pitched on a sandy hill. This lack of knowledge resulted in many an adventuresome night as they battled powerful gales in an effort to keep their tent from blowing away, possibly even out to sea.

Wilbur's letter was passed on to William Tate. Bill Tate enthusiastically replied:

In answering, I would say that you would find here nearly any type of ground you could wish, you could, for instance, get a stretch of sandy land one mile by five with a bare hill in the center, 80 feet high, not a tree or bush anywhere to break the evenness of the wind current. This in my opinion would be a fine place; our winds are always steady, generally from 10 to 12 miles or velocity per mile.

In closing he said:

"If you decide to try your machine here and come, I will take pleasure in doing all I can for your convenience and success and pleasure and I assure you will find a hospitable people when you come among us"("Miracle" 26). Catherine Albertson says in the foreword to her book *Wings over Kill Devil,* "his (Tate's) reply [. . .] proved the deciding factor in bringing the two brothers to Dare."

It is difficult to know if Bishop Wright had any inkling of his sons' intentions, but we can assume he had heard many of their heated discussions when he was home. But he may not have known how serious they were about testing their ideas. In a letter dated September 3, Wilbur told his father he was taking up the investigation of flight for "pleasure rather than profit." He hoped to advance the field of knowledge, if not achieve final success. "At any rate," he concluded, "I shall have had an outing of several weeks and see a part of the world I have never before visited" ("Miracle" 27). He does not even mention the possibility of Orville going.

That was left to Katharine. She wrote her father several days later assuring him that Wilbur would not be reckless. And by the way, "Orv will go down as soon as Will gets the machine ready." We don't know what the good bishop thought about the letters, but he must have wondered what his two sons were doing. Yet, he had raised them to make careful choices and had confidence in their good judgment, so he seems to have simply accepted this new adventure of theirs.

If he had known just what was happening to Wilbur about the time he received the letters, the bishop might have been more concerned. His son was having the time of his life. He boarded the train in Dayton at 6:30 on Thursday evening, September 6, 1900. The next evening he arrived at Old Point Comfort and departed on the steamer, *Pennsylvania,* headed for Norfolk, Virginia. Saturday morning it was hot and muggy in Norfolk, but he had to locate the eighteen-foot-long spruce boards he needed for the biplane. After trying at several lumberyards, he realized he would have to settle for the longest boards he could find, sixteen feet. And these were white pine, not the spruce he intended to use.

When he boarded the train for Elizabeth City, a town forty miles from Kitty Hawk, he must have been exhausted both from the extreme heat and his lack of sleep. At 4:30 p.m. he arrived in Elizabeth City. It was September 8. He checked into the Arlington Hotel and then visited the docks to arrange passage across Albemarle Sound. He discovered no one there had even heard of Kitty Hawk. He had come halfway across the country and was forty miles short of his destination only to discover those living closest to the area didn't even know of Kitty Hawk's existence. He had received two letters with a Kitty Hawk postmark, so he was certain that it did exist and continued to search for a boat to carry him there.

Finally, on Tuesday afternoon, he located Israel Perry, captain of the schooner, *Curlicue.* It was anchored in the Pasquotank River, seven miles away.

That evening Wilbur loaded his trunk and lumber on a tiny skiff and headed up river to the schooner. The skiff was in poor repair and needed constant bailing. Wilbur was hopeful the schooner would be better. In fact, it was in worse shape. Wilbur writes, "The sails were rotten, the ropes badly worn and the rudderpost half rotted off, and the cabin was so dirty and vermin-infested that I kept out of it from first to last" (Kirk 30).

Once out into the sound, the weather changed, the wind intensified, and the waves mounded, causing not only a great concern, but also a great deal of bailing as water swept over the bow of the schooner. Wilbur described the ordeal:

In a severe gust the foresail was blown loose from the boom and fluttered leeward with a terrible roar. The boy and I finally succeeded in taking it in though it was rather dangerous work in the dark with the boat rolling so badly. . . . The mainsail also tore loose from the boom and shook fiercely in the gale. The only chance was to make a straight run over the bar under nothing but a jib, so we took in the mainsail and let the boat swing round stern to the wind. This was a very dangerous maneuver in such a sea but was in some way accomplished without capsizing. [. . .] Israel had been so long a stranger to the touch of water upon his skin that it affected him very much" (Kirk.31).

It was impossible to continue sailing under those conditions, so Captain Perry sought safe haven in the waters of North River. There they remained until the weather cleared the following day.

Wilbur declined to eat Captain Perry's "hash" not because of snobbishness but because he feared for his health. He chose instead to sustain himself by eating Katharine's jar of jam.

Repairs were made to the *Curlicue* and Wednesday afternoon they headed to Kitty Hawk. By the time they reached Kitty Hawk Bay, it was 9:00 in the evening; Wilbur decided it would be better to remain on board until the following morning.

CHAPTER TEN

A KITTY HAWK ADVENTURE

Once Wilbur was on shore he inquired of the young boy, Elijah Baum, the whereabouts of Captain Tate's house. Elijah was a neighbor of the Tate's and took Wilbur straight to the captain's home.

Although Bill Tate had graduated from Atlantic Collegiate Institute in Elizabeth City, he was accustomed to the informality of life on the Outer Banks and must have been surprised at the formal appearance and manners of this young man from the Midwest.

When he heard Wilbur's harrowing tale about his experience on board the *Curlicue* and learned of his lack of food, his heart went out to this young stranger. He and his wife, Addie, sprang into action. The wood in the kitchen stove was rekindled and a proper Outer Banks breakfast was prepared. Tate reported later, "Mr. Wright was seated and done a he-man's part by that humble breakfast. I didn't ask him if he enjoyed it - that question would have been superfluous. Actions speak louder than words, you know" (Kirk 33).

Wilbur had one more request to make of the Tates. Could he stay with them until Orville arrived with their tent?

This called for a family conference. Bill and Addie went into the next room to discuss the matter. Addie was concerned that Wilbur would be dissatisfied with their humble fare. Having overheard their conservation, Wilbur assured them that he would live as they did. The matter was settled. The only request Wilbur made was to ask for a pitcher of boiled water each morning. After Orville's ordeal with typhoid fever, all the Wrights were concerned about the safety of their drinking water. Bill Tate would prove himself to be a gentleman and life-long friend to the Wrights. Steve Kirk calls him one of the legitimate heroes of the Wrights' story.

When Wilbur started assembling his glider in the Tates' front yard, it was clear to them that he felt right at home. Addie loaned him her sewing machine so he could make the adjustments to the French sateen covering for the machine. She may have even helped with some of the sewing.

By the time Orville arrived on September 28, Wilbur had the glider fully assembled. Although Orville had brought all the camping equipment, it wasn't until October 4 that they actually set up camp. By then, Wilbur was well aware of the gusty gales on the Outer Banks so they did take one extra precaution: they anchored their tent to a lowly wind-swept tree. Orville tells of the Kitty Hawkers

1900 GLIDER FLOWN AS A KITE

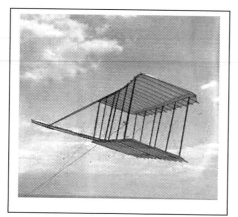

peering around the edge of the woods and out of their upstairs windows to see if they had survived the latest storm.

Wilbur said in his lecture to the engineers that the glider was 165 square feet in area and could be flown in a 21 mile per hour wind. He noted:

On the very day that the glider was completed the wind blew from 25 to 30 miles per hour, and we took it out for trial as a kite. We found that, while it was supported with a man on it in a wind of about 25 miles, its angle was much nearer 20 degrees than 3 degrees. [. . .] As winds of 30 miles per hour are not plentiful on clear days . . . our plan of practicing by the hour, day after day, would have to be postponed. Our system of twisting the surfaces to regulate lateral balance was tried and found to be much more effective than shifting the operator's body. [. . .] When the wind was too light to support the machine with a man on it; we tested it as a kite, working the rudders by cords reaching to the ground. The results were very satisfactory; yet we were well aware that this method of testing is never wholly convincing until the results are confirmed by actual gliding experience (Papers 1: 105).

While Wilbur's description of their initial experience is very factual, many years later Orville told John McMahon, author of *The Wright Brothers: Fathers of Flight,* a livelier version. In this version, Orville and Bill Tate were manning the ropes and Wilbur was riding on the glider. When the glider had ascended about fifteen feet and started to bob up and down, Wilbur panicked and began to holler, "Let me down! Let me down!" The two men immediately pulled hard on the ropes and the glider returned to solid ground. Wilbur's only explanation was, "I promised Pop I'd take care of myself."

In his letters to Katharine, Orville conveys some of the flavor of their unique experiences that summer. He wrote on October 14, 1900:

We are having a fine time. Although we have had the machine out on three different days. . . . The machine seemed a rather docile thing, we taught it behave fairly well. Chains were hung on it to give it work to do, while we took measurements of the 'drift' in pounds.

Well, after erecting a derrick from which to swing our rope with which we fly the machine, we sent it up 20 feet, at which height we attempt to keep it by the manipulation of the strings to the rudder. The greatest difficulty is keeping it down. It naturally wants to go higher and higher.

After an hour or so of practice in steering, we laid it down on the ground to change some of the adjustments of the rope, when without a sixteenth of a second's notice, the wind caught under one corner, and quicker than a thought, it ended 20 feet away a complete wreck" ("Miracle" 33).

Orville's many observations of Outer Banks living are often quite humorous and yet he seemed to appreciate the uniqueness of this remote island. He wrote:

> The poor cows have such a hard time scraping up a living that they don't have time for making milk. You never saw such poor pitiful looking creatures as the horses, hogs and cows down here. The only things that thrive and grow fat are the bedbugs, mosquitoes, and wood ticks. [. . .] [But] this is great country for fishing and hunting. The fish are so thick you see dozens of them whenever you look down into the water. [. . .] The sunsets are the prettiest I have ever seen. The clouds light up in all colors, in the background, with deep blue clouds of various shapes fringed with gold before. [. . .] We certainly can't complain of the place. We came down here for wind and sand, and we have them (Stick 200-203).

On the last day of testing they took the glider four miles south to Kill Devil Hills, which was 100 feet high. Wilbur was able to make his longest glide yet.

The brothers were extremely pleased with the results of their experiments. Wilbur explained in his talk to the engineers:

> Setting out as we did, with almost revolutionary theories on many points and an entirely untried form of machine, we considered it quite a point to be able to return without having our pet theories completely knocked in the head by the hard logic of experience and our brains dashed out in the bargain. Everything seemed to confirm the correctness of our original opinions; (1) that practice is the key to the secret of flying; (2) that it is practicable to assume the horizontal position; (3) that a smaller surface set at a negative angle in front of the main bearing surfaces, or wings, will largely counteract the effect of the fore and aft travel of the center of pressure; (4) that steering up and down can be attained with a rudder without moving the position of the operator's body; (5) that twisting the wings so as to present their ends to the wind at different angles is a more prompt and efficient way of maintaining lateral equilibrium than shifting the body of the operator (Papers 1: 107).

When the Wrights left Kitty Hawk in 1900, they bequeathed their glider to Bill Tate to use as he saw fit. Salvaging shipwrecks and houses was common practice on the Outer Banks. That was just what Tate did. He salvaged every usable part, even the sateen wing covering, which Addie washed, ironed and used to make dresses for their two young daughters, Irene and Pauline.

When the Wrights left the Outer Banks, they carried with them many memories of their unique experiences on that tiny strip of sand protruding out into the Atlantic Ocean. The world was forever changed as a result of their trip to Kitty Hawk, North Carolina.

CHAPTER ELEVEN

ALOFT AGAIN

Although the 1900 trip had been a huge success, major problems still existed. The Wrights knew the 1900 glider lacked the expected lift.

Shortly after their return to Dayton, Wilbur again wrote Chanute telling him about both the successes and failures of their experiments. Chanute, trusting to conventional wisdom, suggested their difficulties might be due to the curvature of the wings. He recommended they use Lilienthal's wing curvature and figure the highest point of their wing based on a arc of an inch rise to every twelve inches of wing from front to back.

The brothers attempted to figure a more accurate curvature. Their experiments, however, failed to produce any satisfactory results, so they accepted Chanute's advice and adopted the curvature of one to twelve. Yet they were concerned because they suspected this ratio was not correct.

They carefully began to design their new craft. It was 22 feet from wingtip to wingtip and 7 feet from front to back. The wing curvature was one-twelfth of the cord (front to back width of the wing). The square footage of the wing surface was 290 square feet. This was the largest glider ever flown up to that time.

With each discussion their enthusiasm built. They were anxious to get back to Kitty Hawk to test their glider. They even hoped to find someone to run the bicycle business so they could pursue their "hobby." They remained open in the evening to accommodate late customers. One hot muggy night in June, a friend, Charlie Taylor, stopped in to chat. Taylor was a gifted mechanic who worked for Dayton Electric. The Wrights offered him a raise of five cents an hour to work for them. Charlie liked the raise plus the fact that he could cycle home for lunch, so he accepted the offer. Little did Taylor suspect that act guaranteed him a permanent place in the history of flight.

A short time later, Wilbur wrote Octave Chanute saying that he and Orville would leave for Kitty Hawk in early July. Chanute made a hasty trip to Dayton. The young brothers must have been in awe of this renowned engineer and chronicler of aeronautic activities. But it wasn't long before all three men were absorbed in an animated conversation. The brothers discussed with Chanute all the details of their 1900 glider and its performance plus their plans for this new glider. By the time Chanute boarded his afternoon train for Tennessee, he was planning to visit the brothers in Kitty Hawk to see for himself their new machine's performance.

Later Chanute wrote the Wrights offering them the services of Edward Huffaker, a protégé, who was building him a glider, and a young doctor, George Spratt, who recently had been corresponding with him. The Wrights reluctantly agreed to have them in camp more as a courtesy to Chanute than to fill any need they themselves had.

The trip started out horrendously. Violent winds, 93 miles per hour, battered eastern North Carolina. In was impossible to attempt a crossing of the Albemarle Sound in such winds. The brothers had to wait in Elizabeth City for several more days until the danger of crossing the sound had passed.

On July 10 the winds had subsided enough for the brothers to cross the Albemarle Sound safely. They arrived on the barrier island at night and spent the evening in Kitty Hawk with the Tates. In the morning, using a borrowed beach cart, they drove the lumber and supplies four miles south to Kill Devil Hills. It was pouring rain when they finally pitched their tent.

Located in *The Papers of Wilbur and Orville Wright* is a letter Orville wrote Katharine:

After fooling around all day inside the tent, excepting on a few occasions when we rushed out to drive a few more tent pegs, our thirst became unbearable, and we decided upon driving the Webbert pump, no well where we could get water being within a mile's distance. Well (pun), we got no well; the point came loose down in the sand and, we lost it! Oh misery! Most dead for water and none within a mile! Excepting what was coming from the skies. However, we decided to catch a little of this, and placed the dish pan where water dripped down from the tent roof; and though it tasted somewhat of the soap we had rubbed on the canvas to keep it from mildewing, it pretty well filled a long-felt want. [. . .]

We continued our well driving all day Saturday, and Sunday spent the day in making a trip to Kitty Hawk (four miles) and in reading. Sunday night I was taken sick and 'most died, that is, I felt as if I did; and managed to keep Will up the best part of the night. The next day I was all right, and we commenced to work on our building (73).

That summer the brothers treated their glider with more respect. They gave it a home. The hanger was an ingenious structure, 16 x 25 x 7 feet high at the eaves. It had hinged doors at either end which could be raised and used as awnings to provide shade and to let the ocean breezes blow through.

Edward Huffaker arrived at the Kill Devil Hills camp the following week "and with him a swarm of mosquitoes, which came in a mighty cloud, almost darkening the sun," Orville wrote in the same letter to Katharine (73).

Orville felt the agonies of the mosquito invasion far surpassed the torments of his typhoid fever ordeal. They ate through socks and underwear, causing painful bites all over the body. The campers rolled up in blankets, but so much perspiration rolled off their bodies that they had to uncover, only to be attacked again by those ferocious winged predators. Their next strategy was to begin burning old tree stumps, then they had to contend with the billowing smoke, which blew in their faces and filled their lungs.

In spite of the torrential rains, the blistering mid-summer's heat and the attack of the vicious mosquitoes, they finally were able to assemble the new glider.

As if their experiences hadn't been bad enough, their July 28 trial of the new glider revealed major control problems. With Wilbur aboard, it stalled. He had to scoot forward to the front edge, but this still failed to compensate for the lack of balance. The machine fell flat on the sand. Will was quite shaken up, but otherwise unharmed. It was this kind of accident that had led to Lilienthal 's death. The front rudder had saved Wilbur from a similar fate. The brothers were perplexed. They understood they had a control problem but they didn't know what was causing it.

Later Wilbur explained to the engineers:

For several days we were in a state of indecision, but were finally convinced by observing the following phenomena: (1) We had removed the upper surface from the machine and were flying it in a wind to see at what angles it would be supported in winds of different strengths. We noticed that in light winds it flew in an upper position [. . .] with a strong upward pull on the cord. As the wind became stronger the angle of incidence (the angle at which the airplane and the wind actually meet) became less, and the surface flew [. . .] with a slight horizontal pull; but when the wind became still stronger it took the lower position [. . .] with a strong downward pull. It at once occurred to me that here was the answer to our problem, for it is evident that in the first case the center of pressure was in front of the center of gravity, and thus pushed up on the front edge; in the second case they were in coincidence (exact same position in space) and the surface in equilibrium (balance), while in the third case the center of pressure had reached a point even behind the center of gravity, and there was therefore a downward pull on the cord. This point having been definitely settled, we proceeded to truss down the ribs of the whole machine, so as to reduce the depth of the curvature.

On resuming our gliding, we found that the old conditions of the preceding year had returned, and after a few trials made a glide of 366 feet and soon after one of 389 feet. The machine with its new curvature never failed to respond promptly to even the small movements of the rudder. The operator could cause it to almost skim the ground, following the undulations of its surface, or he could cause it to sail out almost on a level with the starting point, and passing high above the foot of the hill, gradually settle down to the ground. [. . .] The control of the machine seemed so good that we then felt no apprehension in sailing boldly forth (Papers 1: 110).

Little did Wilbur suspect that more troubles were on the horizon. Orville years later in his court deposition said that they then encountered a new phenomenon. When they attempted to use the wing warping system for more than a brief period, other problems developed. The wing with the greater angle lifted but lost speed and the machine began to spin in a circle forcing the pilot to land abruptly.

From this phenomenon we were led to the discovery that the relative velocities of the right and left wings of the machine bore a very important part in lateral equilibrium, a fact apparently never before considered by any investigators ("Invented" 38).

When they began to fly the machine as a kite and take measurements of lift and drift at various angles of incidence Orville reported that:

The results obtained did not agree at all with the estimated values computed from Lilienthal and other accepted tables of air pressure. [. . .] We also made measurements with the machine flying as a kite, sometimes empty and sometimes loaded with a bag of sand. These measurements show a lift of about one-third of the estimates that had been made using the Lilienthal tables of air pressure ("Invented" 35, 39).

THE 1901 GLIDER

If the Wrights were experiencing a series of difficulties with their experiments, Huffaker's experiment with the cardboard glider funded by Chanute was a catastrophe. The torrential downpours had reduced the glider to a heap of trash. It never got off the ground. But Huffaker wasn't dismayed by this failure. He apparently was awed by the Wright glider and was extremely complimentary when talking to Chanute about it.

But the brothers were not impressed with Huffaker, who offended them by his lack of common courtesy and respect toward their personal things. He often borrowed without asking and failed to help with the work involved in running the camp.

George Spratt, the young doctor from Coatsville, Pennsylvania, on the other hand, was considered a real asset. His funny stories amused and delighted the brothers. He was a self-educated botanist and told them the names of many of the island plants. They continued to correspond with him for many years after their camping experiences together.

Both Spratt and Huffaker had suggested that some of the difficulties might be due to the backward travel of the center of pressure on the curved surfaces at small angles of incidence. They discovered this was true when they flew only one wing as a glider. By the time Chanute arrived at camp, the Wrights had solved the pitch problem, and the glider was back in service by August 8. The new machine with its new curvature responded promptly to the smallest movements of the rudder.

Then they discovered that the wing warping was only effective for brief periods. If used longer it caused the machine to turn towards the wing with the most surface in the air. On August 9, the machine plunged into the sand. Wilbur was thrown forward through the elevator. He walked away with bruises and cuts on his face; the machine laid wrecked in the sand.

The Wrights were still struggling with the problem when Chanute left two days later. When it started to rain again, the Wrights packed up and headed for home. They were understandably disheartened by this lack of progress. Wilbur complained to Orville, "Not within a thousand years would man ever fly." It was a very discouraging time for them. They had no idea at this time just how close they were to solving the major problems with manned flight.

CHAPTER TWELVE

BRIDGING THE GAP

After considering the time, money and energy they had already invested in their pursuit of flight, the Wrights were beginning to believe that all their efforts had been in vain. But Octave Chanute knew better. He knew the Wrights were well ahead of other experimenters in both their thinking and practical application.

At this low point in their career, the genius of Octave Chanute shone through. Whether he wanted to show off his new protégé, get some credit from their work for himself or just wanted to share new information is not known. We do know his invitation to Wilbur to speak to the most prestigious group of engineers in the country was a major turning point for the brothers.

Wilbur had decided to refuse the invitation, but his sister Katharine knew this was a golden opportunity for him and urged him to reconsider, and he did. In preparation for his talk, Wilbur evaluated the progress he and Orville had made, he reviewed the data they had gathered during their experiments and organized that information into a comprehensive whole. In the process, Wilbur came to the same conclusion as Chanute. They were, indeed, well ahead of their contemporaries in both theory and practical application.

On September 18, Wilbur journeyed to Chicago in borrowed apparel. Orville was the better dresser and had loaned Wilbur his dress shirt (complete with collar, cuffs and cuff links) and his overcoat. Katharine was so impressed with Wilbur's appearance that she wrote her father "you never saw Will look so 'swell'" (Papers 1: 99). We have no idea if the clothes created a good impression at the meeting, but we do know his talk made quite an impact on those who heard him. His lecture was published in the *Journal of the Western Society of Engineers* in December 1901, but the published article was not quite as critical of available air pressure tables as Wilbur's presentation had been.

In the process of evaluating their work and analyzing data for Wilbur's lecture, the brothers regained their enthusiasm, but they also began questioning the accuracy of the air pressure tables currently in use. They were committed to finding precise information to use in constructing their flying machine. They required reliable information to calculate the exact dimensions of their machine and to anticipate its performance. The Wrights had used the coefficient of .005 as the coefficient for air pressure under standard atmospheric pressure just as Lilienthal and Chanute had done. But it occurred to Wilbur that perhaps the poor performance of the gliders might be due to using an air pressure coefficient that was too high. He wrote Chanute on September 26, 1901, "While I have not personally tested the point, I am firmly convinced that it [.005] is too high" (Papers 1: 121).

Orville had been concerned about Wilbur's speech. How could they challenge existing data without presenting proof of the errors? Shortly after Wilbur's speech in Chicago, the brothers started conducting a series of experiments to verify the accuracy of Lilienthal 's tables and, if necessary, develop their own figures. Without those experiments they would have progressed no farther than their contemporaries in their pursuit of flight.

They began with a tiny wing and a flat metal plate mounted on a bicycle rim, which they exposed to the wind. The natural wind was not sufficient for lift, so they mounted the rim in front of the handlebars of the bicycle and began pedaling back and forth to create a wind of 27 miles per hour. They wanted to know at what angle the wing would balance the air pressure on the small metal plate. The angle at which the wing balanced the air pressure was 18 degrees, not the five degrees shown on Lilienthal's table. Knowing that they needed more precise information, they made a balancing vane consisting of a vertical rod around which the tiny wing and flat plate rotated. The balance was placed in a wooden trough made from a starch box. A fan was used to create wind. They recorded the difference of the pressure on the metal plate and the lift of the curved surface.

They were so pleased with their results that they made their first wind tunnel, hoping to gain accurate information for constructing a flying machine. They made a wooden box sixteen inches square by six feet long with a viewing window at the top. Wind was created by a fan and funneled into the box through a cone and straightened with a honeycombed piece of sheet metal. The Wrights constructed two balances with which they used to gather their data. One balance provided data for figuring the lift coefficient and the other balance gave them the data necessary to calculate the correct drag coefficient.

TO MEASURE
LIFT: DRIFT

WIND TUNNEL

The brothers tested about one hundred and fifty small wings. Each wing was put through fourteen angles of attack. Once these tests were completed, they unbolted the lift balance and bolted down the drag balance to begin testing the lift to drag ratio.

They discovered which wing curvatures were most effective at different angles to the wind. They learned where the highest curve of a wing needed to be and what was the relationship of the wing's width to its span. Other questions they answered were what the curve of the upper and lower wings should be and what shape to make the wing's leading edge.

Others have said this was the Wrights' best work. Orville said, "Wilbur and I could hardly wait for morning to come to get at something that interested us. *That's* happiness!" (Miller, 60).

There is little doubt that the brothers' healthy skepticism for scientific data, their courage in verifying data, and discarding inaccurate information and then establishing their own sets of figures, was the basis of their ultimate success. Without this ability to question and test their hypotheses, they never would have achieved flight.

Buoyed by their success, the brothers began to design a new machine, their third glider. They had intensely scrutinized every aspect of their work. They now possessed the most accurate figures possible for calculating the dimensions of their new machine. Fred Kelly noted in his biography "that by disregarding all the tables of air pressure used by their predecessors and building according to the figures obtained from their wind tunnel experiments the Wrights made a big advance towards flight" (80).

Katharine wrote Bishop Wright, "The flying machine is in the process of making. Will spins the sewing machine by the hour while Orv squats around marking the places to sew. There is no place in the house to live [. . .]" (Young and Fitzgerald 44). When one considers the dimensions of the new glider, it is not surprising that the "Pride of the West" muslin they used for the wing covering was quite literally taking up much of the living space in the house.

The brothers no longer relied on the work of others. The new glider was truly their own. They used figures calculated from the wind tunnel experiments to design the new machine. The wingspan was six times the width from front to back or 32 feet. In order to achieve better aerodynamics, they varied the wing curvature from 1:24 to 1:30. To provide greater lift, they changed the shape of the forward rudder from a rectangle to an ellipsoid with pointed ends. Then, they added a six-foot twin fin tail. The glider was 16 feet long and weighted 112 pounds. It looked more like a modern aircraft that either of the previous gliders.

At the time, they did not change the operation of the wing warping mechanism. It was still operated by the sideways movement of the pilot in the hip cradle on the lower wing.

The final construction of the glider was postponed until their return to the camp in Kill Devil Hills where they would have room to assemble it.

Meanwhile Wilbur continued to correspond with Chanute, sharing with him the results of the wind tunnel experiments. Chanute offered to calculate the new figures for each form of surface that the Wrights had tested. Wilbur sent him the initial results, but then asked him to wait until they retested. Chanute had already calculated new figures, which he sent to Wilbur.

Several years earlier, in 1896, Chanute had designed two gliders, a multiple-wing glider and a double-decker glider. Augustus Herring tested those gliders for Chanute on the sand dunes in Indiana. Chanute wanted to retest the gliders and to build and test another glider. He had contracted with Charles Lamson in California to construct the new folding wing glider. He asked the Wrights to rebuild the two 1896 gliders and to test all three gliders when they returned to Kill Devil Hills. As a courtesy to Chanute, the Wrights reluctantly agreed to supervise the construction of the earlier two gliders. However, when Augustus Herring asked Chanute if he could build the older models and test them, Chanute reconsidered his agreement with the Wrights. He wrote to Wilbur asking if they would agree to an arrangement where Herring would build the gliders and test them at the Wright camp. Wilbur replied, "To tell the truth, the building of machines for other men to risk their necks is not a task that I particularly relish" (Howard 40).

When Chanute offered the machines to the Wrights as a gift to fly at Kitty Hawk, Wilbur declined. The Wrights wanted to build their own machine using the information from their wind tunnel experiments.

Chanute brought up the issue again when he visited the Wrights in Dayton on July 3. When they again refused, Chanute asked if Herring or Bill Avery could test his gliders at their Kitty Hawk camp. Wilbur responded in a letter that he and Orville had been able to accomplish more alone the previous summer than when others had been in the camp. But if they were given enough time to do some preliminary testing, they would welcome Chanute and his "expert" as their guests. Wilbur also said he would prefer Mr. Avery as the choice of expert.

Although the Wrights conceded to Octave Chanute's request to use their camp as a base to test his gliders, they were not happy about it. These incidents may have been the beginning of a split in their relationship with him. Wilbur continued to correspond with Chanute until 1910, but at times the relationship was quite strained.

CHAPTER THIRTEEN

GLIDING AGAIN

It was during this same period that Bishop Wright became concerned about the management of funds by the publisher of the church paper. He asked Wilbur to examine the account books. After meticulously going over the figures, Wilbur concluded that his father was right; funds had been misappropriated. Bishop Wright and Wilbur wrote three pamphlets explaining the situation to members of the congregations. When Bishop Wright brought the case to court, it was dismissed and he was disciplined for not settling the matter out of court. In the spring of 1902, Wilbur traveled to Huntington, Indiana, to offer evidence in support of his father.

Although raised by a member of the clergy, the brothers did not attend church as adults. They did live the Christian ethic. They gave moral support to their father in his times of trial and provided a home for him in his old age. They refrained from work on Sundays. Wilbur donated a stained glass window to a church in Millville, Indiana. They showed concern for the safety of their flying exhibition team by refusing to let them perform dangerous stunts. They were scrupulously honest and were cautious in expressing feelings that would be hurtful to others, as in the situation mentioned earlier with Octave Chanute. If these facts can be considered objectively, it can be said that they lived as they believed.

Wilbur's efforts on behalf of his father delayed the brothers' return to the Outer Banks for the testing of their glider.

Katharine was concerned for the health of her brothers. She wrote her father on August 20, 1902, "Will is thin and nervous and so is Orv. They will be all right when they get down in the sand where the salt and breeze blow. [. . .] They think life at Kitty Hawk cures all ills, you know" (Fitzgerald and Young 44).

The brothers left for Kitty Hawk on August 25, 1902. They rode the train to Elizabeth City where they arrived at 6:00 p.m. the following evening. When they discovered that Captain Franklin Midgett's schooner, *Lou Willis,* was scheduled to leave before dawn, they rushed back to the train station to retrieve their gliding equipment and personal possessions, which were locked in the baggage room. After loading these items on the schooner, they hurried to make several purchases from the local merchants. At the Standard Oil Company they bought a barrel of oil. Orville persuaded a reluctant storekeeper to reopen his store in order to buy a portable stove. At the grocery store they found the cans of baking soda Orville needed for baking biscuits. It was well after dark when they boarded the schooner exhausted, but excited about testing their new glider.

The schooner departed before dawn. The wind had died to a dead calm and by afternoon they had traveled only ten miles. Captain Midgett tied up for the night. Both the eating and sleeping accommodations were limited. Orville slept on top of a stack of lumber and reported that he "found the more he saw the less he ate" (Kirk 110). When they finally arrived in Kitty Hawk Bay, Dan Tate, half brother of Bill Tate, carried them to their Kill Devil Hills camp in his spritsail.

Their first view of the camp building was a shock. The strong winds of the Outer Banks had removed the sand from beneath both ends of the building, giving the roof "a shape like that of a dromedary's back," Wilbur said in a letter to Chanute. The following day they raised both ends of the shed and supported them with wooden pilings. Then they added a living room and kitchen to the rear. Their new sleeping quarters were beds hung under the roof.

In order to have good water, they dug a well sixteen feet deep. In their absence mice had invaded the shed, making it necessary for them to reestablish their dominance. They also had to chase away the razorback hogs that had taken up residence at their campsite.

With their domestic chores completed, they were free to concentrate on the construction of the new glider. It was September 15 before the wings were ready for testing. Five days later they had finished fifty successful glides.

Up to that time, Wilbur had done all the gliding. Satisfied with the performance of the new glider, he began to teach Orville how to operate it. All was not smooth sailing for Orville. He had made four flights when he noticed one wing getting too high. When he tried to bring the wing back to its normal position, he may have worked the wing warping apparatus the wrong way, because he suddenly found himself descending backwards toward the ground. He reported to Katharine, "The result was a heap of flying machine cloth and sticks with me in the center without a scratch" ("Miracle" 76). Repairs had to be made on the machine before the experiments could continue. But even with this delay, the brothers remained hopeful, their spirits having been lifted by the excellent performance of their new flying machine.

When Chanute's multiple-wing glider arrived on September 24, it had to be carried from the sound across the sand to their camp. Chanute and his "expert" did not come until October 4.

The Wrights were delighted when an unexpected visitor showed up; it was their older brother, Lorin. He had come to see for himself what his two younger brothers were up to. Almost immediately Lorin was put to work running errands, helping with the glider and taking photographs. Wilbur had been able to persuade George Spratt, their friend from Pennsylvania, that the mosquitoes were better this year and so was the water. Spratt came the day after Lorin and the two men became instant friends, fishing, crabbing and hunting together.

Life in the Wright camp was very enjoyable for the time being. The four men enjoyed each other's company and often held long discussions far into the night. New gliding records were set - three glides over 500 feet and five glides between 20 and 30 seconds in duration. Just when everything seemed to be going well, they noticed a new problem. Occasionally when the wing warping was applied, the machine quickly slid sideways towards the low wing, and then the wingtip would strike the sand and bore itself in. This "well digging" or tailspin was very dangerous. It was quite puzzling to the brothers who realized they had not yet perfected control of the glider's flight.

After much debate one evening, the foursome retired, but Orville had consumed a considerable amount of coffee, which caused him to lie awake with his mind racing over the details of the phenomenon. By morning he was convinced he had solved the problem. He gave Lorin a wink to alert him that he had something important to say to Wilbur, but he was sure Wilbur would dismiss it, as usual.

Much to his surprise, Wilbur greeted the news in silence. After some thought, he agreed with Orville that a moveable tail might just solve the problem. However, he was concerned about making the pilot responsible for controlling yet another task. In addition to accepting Orville's idea, he suggested making the functions of wing warping and moving the wing into a single mechanism. Then with one act the pilot could achieve control over both the axes of pitch and yaw.

1902 GLIDER

In their book, *Twelve Seconds to the Moon: Story of the Wright Brothers*, Young and Fitzgerald write: "The modified glider had for the first time control over all three flight motions; wing warping for roll control, elevator [forward rudder] for pitch control, and a single vertical movable rudder for yaw control" (45).

Octave Chanute and Augustus Herring arrived at the Kill Devil Hills camp on October 4. Chanute was anxious to have Herring test his three gliders, the oscillating wing glider built by Lamson and the two built by Herring.

All three gliders failed to meet Chanute's expectations. This must have been the ultimate blow to Chanute's desire to design a successful glider.

For Herring it was very humiliating. He considered himself the premier gliding expert, but now he found himself faced with the success of the Wrights' glider. Two days after the failure of the Chanute gliders, both Chanute and Herring left the camp.

Alone at last, the brothers soared. Orville bragged to Katharine, "we made over 250 glides, or more than we had made all together up to the time Lorin left. We have gained considerable proficiency in the handling of the machine now, so that we are able to take it out in any kind of weather. Day before yesterday we had a wind of 16 meters per second or about 30 miles per hour, and glided in it without any trouble. That was the highest wind a gliding machine was ever in, so that we now hold all the records! The largest machine that we handled in any kind (of weather), made the longest distance glide (American), the longest time in the air, the smallest angle of descent, and the highest wind!!! Well, I'll leave the rest of the "blow" till we get home" (Papers 1: 280).

On October 23 Wilbur set a record of 622.5 feet in 26 seconds; he was followed closely by Orville's flight of 612.5 feet in about 21 seconds.

It is evident in Orville's letter to Katharine that the success of the 1902 glider was exhilarating for both Wilbur and Orville. They had solved the major control problems of flight. Their persistence and precise methods of testing and experimentation had paid off. They were now able to consider powered flight.

BANKING

CHAPTER FOURTEEN

THE FLYER

The Wright brothers felt confident. They anticipated little difficulty constructing a machine built for powered flight. With the 1902 glider, they had demonstrated mastery over the major problems of control. The wing warping mechanism controlled the plane's rotation from side to side (its roll). The elevator controlled the plane's pitch (its up and down movement), and the movable tail controlled the yaw (the side-to-side movement of the plane's nose).

Now they were ready for powered flight, or so they thought. Wilbur wrote several major automobile makers describing the type of engine they needed. It had to be lightweight (less than two hundred pounds), deliver eight horsepower and run smoothly.

Next, they considered the propellers they needed for thrust. Marine propellers had been used on ships for decades. Surely there was plenty of information available for reading. They would simply adapt the information that had been developed for water use to air use.

Much to their surprise, these assumptions were dead wrong. No maker of automobile engines was the least bit interested in constructing an engine for a flying machine. In 1900 anyone who thought a man could fly was considered delusional and someone who proposed to build a flying machine was considered an outright fraud. No respectable businessman wanted to be associated with such an outlandish endeavor. Why, just recently a well-known astronomer, Simon Newcomb, had declared that flying was an impossible dream. Of the many auto manufacturers that Wilbur wrote, only ten responded and not one was willing to build an engine for the flying machine.

But the Wrights were respectable businessmen and they knew deep in their souls that flying was possible. They had already constructed and flown three gliders. They had conducted numerous experiments and developed their own sets of tables correcting many erroneous conceptions held by the experts of their day.

Now that they were ready for powered flight, they were unable to convince the builders of engines that theirs was a legitimate pursuit. So they did the only thing they could. With the help of their talented mechanic, Charlie Taylor, they designed and built their own engine! After all, they had earlier built an internal-combustion engine to drive the line shaft in the bicycle shop.

A local foundry cast the crankcase and four cylinders out of aluminum. Charlie Taylor told of his role in an article written for *Collier's* in 1948.

One of us would sketch out the part we were talking about on a piece of paper and I'd spike the sketch over my bench. It took me six weeks to make that engine. The only metalworking machines we had were a lathe and a drill press, run by belts from a stationary gas engine. [. . .] The fuel system was simple. A one-gallon fuel tank was suspended from a wing strut, and the gasoline fed by gravity down a tube to the engine. [. . .] A simple chain and sprocket wheel drove each of the two propellers. The wheel was attached to the propeller shaft; the chain ran down to the motor. [. . .]

I think the hardest job Will and Orv had was with the propellers. I don't believe they were ever given enough credit for that development. They read up on all that was published about boat propellers, but they couldn't find any formula for what they needed. So they had to develop their own, this they did in the wind tunnel. They concluded that the air propeller was really just a rotating wing and by experimenting in the wind box they got the design they wanted. They made the propellers out of three lengths of wood, glued together at staggered intervals. Then they cut them down to the right size and shape with a hatchet and drawshave. They were good propellers (68).

1903 MOTOR

Years later, Orville wrote an article in *Century Magazine* in which he reported:

What at first seemed a simple problem became more complex the longer we studied it. With the machine moving forward, the air flying backward, the propellers turning sidewise, and nothing standing still, it seemed impossible to find a starting-point from which to trace the various simultaneous reactions. Contemplation of it was confusing. After long arguments we often found ourselves in the ludicrous position of each having been converted to the other's side, with no more agreement than when the discussion began (648).

The brothers filled five notebooks with notations on their theories and formulas. In the end, they constructed propellers that were 8 feet, 6 inches in diameter and had the unprecedented efficiency of 66 per cent. Culick and Dunsmore in *On Great White Wings* state that, "Two thirds of the 12 horsepower reaching the propellers was converted to thrust" (60). The propellers were mounted on the rear of the machine behind the wings. One propeller rotated clockwise and the other rotated counter-clockwise. With this configuration the propellers moved the maximum amount of air to provide the maximum amount of thrust.

The new machine was not the sleek white beauty that the 1902 glider had been. It had to be sturdy enough to carry a 200-pound motor with all its accessories, to have a 140-pound pilot on board and to withstand the powerful thrust of the 8-foot, 6-inch propellers.

In their wind tunnel experiments, they discovered the strut shape which presented the least wind resistance. It was a strut with a rectangular cross section and rounded front and rear edges. These struts were so tightly fitted they had to be forced into place. The landing skids were extended to eliminate the possibility of the machine rolling over. Both the forward rudder and the moveable vertical tail were doubled to provide better control. The top and bottom of the 40-foot, 4-inch wings were covered with "Pride of the West" muslin.

Each wing was made in three sections. The center section was rigidly trussed to support the engine, pilot and drive mechanism. The hip cradle, designed for operating both the wing warping and the vertical tail, was located in the middle section, as was the hand control for the elevator. The outer sections were able to be flexed by the wing warping wires and were lower than the middle sections. In fact they made the wings look like they were drooping. But what the machine lacked in beauty, it more than made up for in sturdiness.

This was a heavy machine. It weighted in at 675 pounds and had a 40-foot, 4-inch wingspan with a 6-foot, 6-inch deep chord (wing width). The propellers rotated in an eight-foot, 6-inch diameter and the engine produced 12 horsepower. It was impressive! But the Wrights wouldn't be able to see just how impressive it was until they assembled it on the Outer Banks of North Carolina in the fall of 1903.

On this machine rested their hopes and their dreams. In spite of all their hard work and thought, the big question still remained. Could it fly?

They knew others were close. Chanute made that clear. They were well aware that Samuel P. Langley, the director of the prestigious Smithsonian Institute, had received over $50,000 from the U.S. Government for his Great Aerodrome. Langley had already demonstrated that a large motorized model could fly. Who would be first - the well-funded, well-placed Langley or the modest Wrights with funds gleaned solely from their bicycle business?

The answer came quickly when Langley attempted a flight the following month. An October 8 report in the *Washington Post* stated that he launched the giant tandem-winged machine from the top of a houseboat on the Potomac River. The 700 pound flying machine dropped into the water "like a stone," carrying with it Charles Manly, the builder and pilot. Later in a letter, Orville commented to Katharine that its surfaces were inefficient and that Langley's assistant had little control over the machine. Wilbur wondered in a letter to Chanute what their luck would be. Neither brother seemed to dwell much on Langley's failure for they had their own trial to prepare.

It was the last week in September 1903, before they were ready to leave for North Carolina. The trip went smoothly until they reached Elizabeth City. There they learned that the freight depot had burned the week before. With much fear and trepidation, they combed through the ruins of the depot. When they failed to find anything that looked like their supplies, they boarded the *Ocracoke* and continued their journey. In Manteo they transferred to Meekins' gasoline launch and headed for Kill Devil Hills and their camp. Much to their relief, they discovered their supplies and lumber were already there.

When Dan Tate, Bill's half brother, first greeted them at the camp, he recounted all the perils that had befallen the Outer Banks' residents since the brothers' last visit. Orville relays some of these details in a letter to Katharine.

Dan says this year has been one continuous succession of storms of unprecedented severity; the rain had descended in such torrents as to make a lake for miles about our camp; the mosquitoes were so thick they turned day into night, and the lightning so terrible that it turned night into day. Really it paralyzes the mind to think of all these things at once. Besides all those, the sun was so hot, it must have made soup out of the mosquitoes and rain! (Papers 1: 357).

After hearing Tate's rendition of the horrendous weather the Banks residents had been enduring in their absence, the brothers understood why their camp building was now standing two feet nearer the ocean, minus its foundation. Once they restored the building to its foundation, Orville set up the kitchen and experimented with eliminating the use of eggs in clarifying their coffee by making a "French Drip" coffee pot.

In Orville's letter to Katharine on September 26, he explained their plan of taking out the old machine on windy days and working on the new machine on rainy and calm days. He reported the hills were in the best shape for gliding and optimistically declared that things were starting off more favorably than in other years.

The brothers had planned to start their new shed early on Monday morning but the weather was so fine they postponed the shed until after they had a chance to spend the morning gliding. The new shed was big enough to accommodate the dimensions of the powered machine when it was fully assembled. It was 44 feet long x 16 feet wide x 9 feet high.

True to Orville's prediction, whenever the weather was windy enough, the brothers went gliding. Wilbur wrote Chanute: "Our glides are higher and more spectacular than any heretofore" (Papers 1: 360). The brothers not only repeated their earlier successes, but also set many new records. But their gliding time was severely interrupted by the fall storm season bringing with it heavy winds, drenching rain and bitter cold.

Wilbur described a storm, which apparently took place on Thursday, October 8. He stated that it was such a cloudburst that it cost them sleep that night. The storm got much worse the next day. It reached hurricane strength with winds of 75 miles per hour. Orville ventured forth to repair the roof before it blew away. He donned Wilbur's overcoat, grabbed the ladder and headed into the storm. But instead of climbing up to the roof as he planned, the wind pushed him backwards until he was fifty feet from the building. Wilbur saw he needed to assist, so he ventured out. He discovered that his brother was now at the side of the building trying to get the ladder up. Finally, Orville was able to climb to the roof with Wilbur holding the ladder for him. Once on the roof, the wind lifted the overcoat over his head. He was now unable to reach either, his hammer and nails or to pull his coat down. So he retreated backward down the ladder. This time he put the nails in his mouth and held the hammer in his hand. He ascended the ladder again and attempted to nail down the loose tarpaper, but the wind was so powerful he missed the nail more often than he hit it. Both brothers got thoroughly soaked but the job finally got done. Wilbur noted that the storm continued through the night, so they took the advice of the Oberlin coach who had said, "Cheer up, boys there is no hope," and went to bed where they slept soundly. Wilbur wrote, "The storm continued through Saturday and Sunday, but by Monday it had reared up so much that it finally fell over on its back and lay quiet" (Papers 1: 367).

The bitter cold weather provided a different challenge for the Wrights. Wilbur wrote another letter to his father and Katharine addressing this subject:

> In addition to [. . .] 1, 2, 3, and 4 blankets nights, we now have 5 blanket nights, & 5 blankets & 2 quilts. Next come 5 blankets, 2 quilts & fire; then 5, 2, fire, & hot-water jug. This is as far as we have got so far. Next comes the addition of sleeping without undressing, then shoes & hats, and finally overcoats. We intend to be comfortable while we are here (Papers 1: 383).

They did indeed mean to be comfortable. When George Spratt arrived on October 23, Orville and George built a wood-burning stove out of an empty carbide can. When they fired it up, it filled the room with soot. Black soot covered every square inch of their living quarters. Now they needed wood to burn.

Their local employee, Dan Tate, was not very handy with tools, so they had him help get the glider up the hill. He wasn't too happy about that even though he was being paid $7 a week, an unheard of amount for an Outer Banker in those days. When the Wrights told him to collect some driftwood for their stove, he quit.

The Wrights had bigger problems facing them than the loss of their handyman. While preparing to test the engine and propellers, they discovered they were unable to tighten the sprockets sufficiently. When the engine kept missing, the vibrations caused the shafts to break. Then the magneto wouldn't produce enough spark to ignite the gas.

When George Spratt saw there was no hope of a flight for at least ten days, if ever, he decided to leave. He took with him the broken propeller shafts to send them to Charlie Taylor in Dayton.

In Manteo, Spratt met Chanute who was just arriving for his visit to the Wrights' camp. George was so distraught over the Wrights difficulties that Chanute had to reassure him that the Wrights were sensible young men and wouldn't do anything foolish.

Thus reassured, Spratt left for home and Chanute proceeded to the Wrights' camp to see for himself what had caused George Spratt such concern.

CHAPTER FIFTEEN

FLYING AT LAST

The cold blustery weather was a severe hardship for Chanute, a man now in his seventies. He stayed only a week. But of even greater concern to him than the cold, was the fact that the Wrights had not left any room for error when they figured the weight, size and power of their new power machine. He said that 30 per cent of the power would be lost in the transmission of that power from the engine to the propellers.

The finished machine weighed seventy pounds more than they figured. So even with the additional four horsepower their engine was producing, there wouldn't be enough thrust to get the machine off the ground. They hoped Chanute was wrong, but they were afraid he just might be right. There was nothing they could do but wait until the new shafts arrived and then attempt to fly. Meanwhile, Orville busied himself with learning French and German.

Sadly, while their improvised carbide can stove provided them with much needed heat, it also dried out the frame of the 1902 glider, making it too "rickety" to be safe. Their last glide seems to have been the middle of October.

By November 19, the ponds around the camp were freezing and at times it was too cold even to work.

When the propeller shafts finally arrived about noon, November 20, the brothers mounted them on the plane and prepared to begin testing again. But then the magneto failed to produce enough spark and the sprockets came loose. The Wrights remembered an adhesive they had brought from the bicycle shop. They had used it to repair other items. Why not give it a try? They filled the threads of the sprocket with Arnstein's Hard Cement and tightened the sprockets. It worked! Now the sprockets were secure but the engine jerked the chains so hard that the whole machine shook violently. They traced the problem to a faulty gasoline valve. They must have been very frustrated because they desperately needed to find out if Chanute was correct in his prediction. Chanute had assumed that there wouldn't be enough thrust to get the plane airborne because 30 per cent of the engine's power would be lost by the time it reached the propellers.

They just had to know, so they contrived an ingenious method of measuring the amount of thrust they had. Orville described their method in his diary:

> After dinner we arranged to measure the thrust by supporting [the] center skids on rollers and fastening one end of [the] machine, while we attached a rope to the other end, which ran over a pulley and carried a 50 lb. box of sand. Besides lifting the sand we got an additional pull of 16 to 18 lbs. on

the scales, which made the total thrust of the [propellers] screws 132 to 136 lbs. at a speed of 350 revolutions per min. Our confidence in the success of the machine is now greater than ever (Papers 1: 384).

Chanute was wrong. The machine would fly! They must have breathed a sigh of relief because now they knew success was possible.

They had to start the plane from level ground, so there would be no question that it was the engine power that provided the thrust needed to launch the plane. The skids prevented the machine from sinking into the sand but they couldn't run on top of the sand. The plane required some sort of runway. The Wrights devised a 60 feet long track, which was made of 15 foot two-by-fours that were set on their sides and had a metal strip running the length of the top. They made a dolly, sometimes referred to as a truck, which consisted of a pair of wheels made from bicycle wheel hubs and connected by a crossbar. On top of the crossbar they screwed a large piece of wood, which looked like an oxen yoke. The skids of the machine rested on that yoke as the dolly rolled down the track. When the plane lifted into the air, the dolly dropped off the track. The entire track was made to be moveable.

What happened next can only be called an unfortunate twist of fate. On Saturday, November 28, while they were testing the speed of the engine and propellers, they encountered still another problem. There was a crack in the propeller shafts.

Orville left for Dayton the following Monday, November 30, to make more durable propeller shafts. He arrived back in Kill Devil Hills on December 11. During his travels, he had read about Langley's second attempt to fly the Great Aerodrome. That time the rear of the engine caught on the launching apparatus and the supporting surface broke off. The huge machine plunged into the icy waters of the Potomac, burying poor Charles Manly beneath the ice. One of his assistants dove into the rigid waters to free him. After nearly losing his life, Manly gave up the pursuit of flight. Samuel Langley wrote a scholarly explanation of the trial, but that was his last attempt to fly. It was up to the Wrights. Many had tried, but no one had yet succeeded.

With new shafts made of spring steel, the Wrights were ready for a trial run, but the weather was uncooperative. As they waited for a more suitable day to make the test flight, they ran the machine along the track, checking all its functions and making sure everything was ready for the trial flight.

With the winter weather rapidly closing in, the brothers had to take advantage of every day when flight was even remotely possible. That may explain why they made an attempt to fly on December 14, even though the wind was too light for a start from level ground. They moved the track and heavy machine to make a downhill start on the big hill. The Wrights needed help setting up and they wanted reliable people to verify that the plane flew.

They notified the members of the Kill Devil Hills lifesaving station by raising a signal flag. Five surf men responded: Bob Westcott, John T. Daniels, Tom Beacham, Will Dough and "Uncle Benny" O'Neal came, along with two young boys and their dog.

It took all seven men forty minutes to get the track laid and the 700 pound machine (Crouch 260) 150 feet up the hill. It was 3:00 before they were able to fire up the engine. Its loud roar of the engine so frightened the two boys and the dog that they ran off as fast as they could go.

The brothers tossed a coin. Wilbur won. He climbed on the machine and lay prone on the lower wing. The weight of the machine held the rope so taut that Wilbur was unable to undo it. The men pushed the machine back up the track until the rope slipped loose. Down the track the machine raced, it rose fifteen feet in the air, slowed down, stopped and then fell to the earth. Wilbur sat motionless, momentarily stunned. The engine was still running and the propellers were still spinning. Finally he reached over and turned off the engine. Several pieces of the plane were broken by the forceful landing.

FALSE START

Howard wrote that:
> Although the Flyer had traveled over 100 feet, The Wright brothers did not consider this a true flight. All the same, they were elated. The test had proved four important things about the untried Flyer. Its strength in flight was satisfying, the motor was reliable, the power sufficient, and the launching system both safe and practical. There was no question of final success (134).

The brothers realized the downhill start compromised their claim for an unassisted powered flight. A day and a half later, after making the necessary repairs to the machine, they laid out the track on level ground, but by the time they finished, the wind had died down. They would have to wait for another day.

When they checked outside the morning of December 17, they found the puddles around camp were frozen solid and a gale blowing across the sandy plain. They dressed as usual in dark suits, white shirts with stiff collars and ties.

The blustery wind was coming from the north and registering 24 miles per hour. They delayed as long as they could.

At 10:00 they raised the signal. Three surfmen came: Adam Etheridge, John Daniels and Will Dough. A lumber buyer from Manteo, W. C. Brinkley, and a teenage boy, Johnny Moore, came also.

By 10:30 all was ready. The Flyer sat poised on top of the dolly, which was ready to roll down the track and drop onto the sand as the plane ascended into the sky. It was now Orville's turn. Wilbur and Orville held a brief conference. Eyewitnesses say that the two brothers clung to each other's hand as if this moment of parting would be the last time they would see the other.

We will never know what passed between the brothers, but clearly emotions ran high. The brothers were acutely aware that other men had lost their lives attempting flight without using power. They were attempting flight using an engine. They knew there was great risk in what they were doing.

They shook hands and Orville walked towards the machine with its engine roaring loudly. He lay prone in the hip cradle on the lower wing and checked the controls, the rudder for ascending and descending, the combination wing warping and vertical tail for sideways maneuvering and the lever which regulated the gasoline flow, released the restraining rope and set in motion the recording devises.

Earlier he had instructed John Daniels on how to take the picture of the first flight. Orville had positioned the camera at just the right place to capture a picture of the plane as it became airborne.

Orville waited until Daniels was in position, then he moved the lever to the far left, releasing the restraining rope. The plane started slowly down the track, and then it picked up speed until it was going eight miles per hour. When it reached the fourth section of track, it ascended ten feet in the air. That first flight was anything but smooth. The gusty wind was probably as much to blame as was the poor rudder control. The plane darted up and down and up and down. Finally it darted straight into the sand. It had traveled 120 feet in 12 seconds. Did the Wrights whoop and holler over their success? There is no mention that they did. But surely they must have felt exhilarated that finally they had achieved sustained powered flight.

For the first time in recorded history an airplane, by its own power and under the control of the pilot, had rolled on a metal-capped wooden track, rose into the air, and landed on the ground at the same elevation from which it started. This was the first time in the history of man that a human had successfully flown a heavier-than-air, powered machine This was indeed man's first small step toward space. That brief flight changed forever the course of human history.

In *How We Made The First Flight*, Orville wrote:
This flight lasted only 12 seconds, but it was nevertheless the first in the history of the world in which a machine carrying a man had raised itself by its own power into the air in full flight, had sailed forward without reduction in speed, and had finally landed at a point as high as that from which it started (Jakab and Young, 47).

THR FIRST HEAVIER THAN AIR POWERED FLIGHT

The Outer Bankers who witnessed this momentous event rushed forward to congratulate Orville. Then they all hauled the heavy machine back to the starting track. After a brief interlude in the Wrights heated living quarters to warm up, they went back out into the rigid weather to try again.

It was Wilbur's turn. The repairs were made quickly and at 11:20 the plane rolled across the track and lifted into the air. The flight was still rough but the distance covered was 175 feet. Once again the machine was hauled back to the starting point and at 11:40 with Orville at the controls, the plane rose 14 feet in the air. A strong gust of wind caught the left wing causing the plane to sidle left. Orville turned the rudder, bringing the plane down 200 feet away from the starting point. Wilbur took the controls again at noon. The machine started acting like a bucking bronco, but at about 200 feet it conceded control to Wilbur. At 800 feet it regained its feisty manner and pitched upward, then suddenly it darted toward the ground. The forward rudder was damaged during the landing. Wilbur had covered 852 feet in 59 seconds. A monumental achievement!

The plane was carried back to camp. As the men talked, a strong wind started to turn the plane over. Orville and John Daniels grabbed its spars. The machine turned over on the men. Daniels got caught inside between the engine and chains. The machine turned over and over. Although Daniels was lucky to escape with just a few bad bruises, the plane wasn't so fortunate. It was badly damaged. The legs of the engine were broken off, the chain guides bent; the rear ends of the ribs, some uprights and a spar were all broken. The plane would never fly again.

The Wrights had to be content with their four powered flights. They knew then they could fly. What delicious delight they must have felt. They had succeeded against all odds.

They ate dinner, then walked the four miles to Kitty Hawk to telegram their father. They knew he would want to know. While in Kitty Hawk they called on friends, Captain and Mrs. Hobbs, Dr. Cogwell and, of course, the lifesavers at the Kitty Hawk station.

The next day they dismantled the machine and packed it in crates for shipping to Dayton. They were going home for Christmas! What a wonderful Christmas gift this was! After so many years of research, triumphs and failures, they had accomplished what no other men ever had. They had flown an airplane for the very first time in human history!

CHAPTER SIXTEEN

REPERCUSSIONS

In all their planning and experimentation, the brothers had been very careful. They tried to avoid mistakes, but they never could have anticipated what happened when Orville sent their father the following telegram.

Success four flights Thursday morning all against 21 mile wind started from level with engine power alone average speed through air 31 miles longest 57 seconds inform Press home Christmas (Papers 1: 397).

As they prepared to leave the Kitty Hawk weather station, a request came from the Norfolk telegraph office asking permission to inform a reporter from the *Virginian-Pilot* about the flights. The Wrights were quite clear; they did not want this information passed on to the Virginia paper.

The brothers had already arranged to have Lorin Wright, their older brother, inform the Dayton press of their exploits. They sent the telegram to their father who was to prepare a brief press release. Katharine was to send a telegram to Chanute and to take the release to Lorin, who would carry it to the Dayton *Journal*. It seemed like a simple plan and it was.

When Carrie Grumbach, the housekeeper, gave the telegram to the bishop, he wrote the press release. When Katharine got home she took the telegram and press release to Lorin's house. Lorin ate his dinner and then went down to the office of the Dayton *Journal*. There the plan fell apart. When Lorin gave the information to Frank Tunison, the local Associated Press representative, Tunison was unimpressed by news of a flight, which lasted only fifty-seven seconds. However, he said if the flight had been 57 minutes, then it would have been a newsworthy.

Lorin was dumbfounded! How could this man fail to realize the importance of what had just occurred? Men had tried for centuries to fly and two men, his brothers, had done just that! They flew a manned, heavier-than-air powered plane!

Many years later, Ivonette Wright, Lorin's daughter, spoke about the dejected expression on her father's face when he returned home.

Even if the Dayton *Journal* wasn't interested in the story, the *Virginian-Pilot* was. Whatever details were missing from the telegram, the editor, Keville Glennan, and the reporter, Edward Dean, conjured up. The headlines for their fantastic tale ran across the top of the front page and stated:

FLYING MACHINE SOARS THREE-MILES IN TEETH OF HIGH WIND OVER SAND HILLS AND WAVES AT KITTY HAWK NORTH CAROLINA.

The whole incident might have been amusing had not the misinformation become a news item in the *New York American* and in Cincinnati's *Enquirer*, which ran the convoluted story the next morning. The Dayton papers finally picked up the Norfolk version of the flights and reported the story without bothering to check the details even though two local boys had accomplished something quite amazing.

The brothers seemed mystified by these fantastic figments of imagination reported in the papers. They were also amused by them. On the way home they sent a wire to Katharine from Huntington, West Virginia stating they had survived the treacherous journey over the ocean reported by the newspapers and would be home that night.

Even before they left Kill Devil Hills they were besieged by requests for pictures and the rights to their story. While still at camp, they received two telegrams from Chanute. In both telegrams he said, "When ready to make public, please inform me" (Papers 1: 399). Chanute seemed to have assumed that he would play some role in publicizing the Wrights' success. It wasn't until months later that Wilbur asked Chanute to inform his friends of their progress.

The Wrights may have been cautious of involving Chanute, because in the spring of 1903 he had given a speech to the Aero Club of France in which he mentioned the Wrights' work and gave the impression that he was advising them. Afterward, Ernest Archdeacon, a member of the club, wrote an article in which he said Mr. Wilbur Wright was one of Chanute's "pupils, capable of carrying on his (Chanute's) researches" (Papers 1: 655). Chanute never corrected this misrepresentation of his relationship with the brothers. In addition, Chanute seems to have included in that speech details of the Wrights' wing warping system. That leakage of information caused the Wrights many difficulties when they tried to protect their European patents. It is impossible to know if Chanute's inclusion of that information was intentional or an oversight on his part. But, it seemed that the once warm relationship enjoyed by Chanute and the Wrights was cooling.

An entry Bishop Wright made in his diary made on December 22 indicated that reporters had also besieged him. That same day he wrote a letter to Carl Dienstbach, a correspondent for a German aeronautical journal, and attempted to clarify some of the misinformation contained in the Norfolk dispatch. But the bishop, too, muddied the waters by the statements he made. He mentioned that his sons laid the track downhill but they started from level ground. He said no flight exceeded a thousand feet in length and, although he did not know the height, he thought it was less than thirty feet. The last paragraph of that letter shone with a father's pride and is well worth reading.

> Wilbur is 36, Orville is 32, and they are as inseparable as twins. For several years they have read up on aeronautics as a physician would read his books, and they have studied, discussed, and experimented together. Natural workmen, they have invented, constructed, and operated their gliders, and finally their "Wright Flyer," jointly, all at their own personal expense. About equal credit is due each (Papers 1: 400).

Famished and exhausted, the brothers arrived at 7 Hawthorne Street at 8:00 pm, December 23. One can only imagine the delight Bishop Wright and

Katharine felt on welcoming the boys home. Carrie Grumbach knew they hadn't had a decent meal in months. She prepared porterhouse steak and a delicious dessert to celebrate their homecoming. She let them know there was plenty more where that came from, but she hadn't planned on Orville's voracious appetite for fresh milk. After seven or eight glasses, she was almost out. When he asked for more, she faced a dilemma. Should she say there wasn't any more or should she try not to disappoint him and just fill the rest of the glass with water? She chose to add the water. One mouthful and he knew. He screamed in protest, saying she had tried to deceive him by "dairying" the milk. To the end of his life he teased her about "dairying" his milk.

The Wright family enjoyed a happy Christmas together. Christmas dinner was at Lorin's. Gifts were given to all. Wilbur and Orville gave Katharine a set of silver forks and pearl-handled steak knives. Charlie Taylor got a two-inch micrometer.

Two days later, Chanute wrote asking Wilbur to speak at the American Association for the Advancement of Science to give an account of their flights. The meeting was to be held in St. Louis, December 28 to Jan 2. Wilbur wired the Chanute; "We are giving no pictures nor descriptions of machine or methods at present" (Papers 1: 401). The following day Wilbur wrote Chanute a long and detailed letter telling him the circumstances that occurred after Chanute's departure from their camp and the particulars of the four successful flights on December 17. He ended the letter with the statement:

> One of the most gratifying features of the trials was the fact that all our calculations were shown to have worked out with absolute exactness so far as we can see, though we have not yet made our final computations on the performance of the machine (Papers 1: 403).

A little dig, perhaps, meant to remind Chanute of his prediction that they would not fly because they hadn't allowed for the loss of power in transmission.

Trouble began to rear its ugly head in the person of A.M. Herring who had tested Chanute's gliders at the Wright camp the year before. In a letter to the Wrights, Herring claims to have independently solved the problem of powered flight and offered to join forces with the Wrights for a third share.

Wilbur never responded to this letter, but he did comment on it both to Spratt and Chanute. Several years later Herring joined forces with Glenn Curtis; eventually the Wrights took him and Curtiss to court for patent infringements.

It wasn't until January 5 that the brothers released to the Associated Press an official statement of their first flights. They clipped copies of this article from the papers and sent them to several interested persons. Chanute did the same thing with a Chicago paper.

Now that the brothers had proved their machine could fly, they needed to secure a U.S. patent for their control system. If they didn't, anyone could copy the system and they would receive no compensation for all the hard work they had done. They had previously applied for one, but were refused. It was suggested they get a patent attorney to file an application for them. They made this their top priority. On January 22, after consulting with several lawyers, they went to Springfield, Ohio, and engaged Mr. H. A. Toulmin. He advised them to get the patent on the soaring machine to avoid having to demonstrate the operation of the power machine in front of judges. He cautioned them about giving out the details of their machine.

With the application for a patent in process, the brothers turned to the development of a new machine. On January 25, Orville took patterns to the foundry for casting the aluminum frame of the new engine.

In writing to a friend, Wilbur spoke of the fork in the road. They had no inkling of what lay ahead, but it was obvious flying was more than a hobby. It was a life pursuit. Whether he and Orville made a conscious decision or were carried along by the momentum of the moment, their life had changed forever with that first successful flight. They would devote their life to the development of a dependable airplane which could be put to practical use. Charles Taylor would repair the bicycles and work on the new Flyer

Earlier Chanute had urged the brothers to get a patent; now he was saying don't bother, it will only be a narrow one and it could easily be challenged. He tried to get the Wrights to capitalize on their publicity and exhibit the plane for the entire world to see. In fact, he knew the perfect place to do this, the upcoming World's Fair, to be held in St. Louis. Chanute was one of the fair's promoters and even had helped to write the rules for the flying competition. The Wrights gave this option serious consideration, but after going over the rules and visiting the competition area, they decided it was much too dangerous for a powered machine.

What they needed then was a level flying field close to home, which they found eight miles outside of Dayton. It was a cow pasture complete with cows, horses and a barbed wire fence. The owner was a local banker, Torrence Huffman, who thought the brothers were fools, but nevertheless granted them permission to use his field as long as they moved the cows and horses before they started flying.

Then they made a bigger and more powerful engine, which weighted 240 pounds when fully fueled. It produced 15-16 horsepower, which eventually increased to 20 horsepower. The wing curvature was changed from 1:20 to 1:25 and the spars were made of white pine instead of spruce. Neither of these two changes proved very satisfactory. In 1905, they went back to the original wing curvature and spruce spars.

To avert the shenanigans of the first media reports, the brothers invited the media to witness the testing of their new plane on May 23, 1904. Calm winds prevented the anticipated demonstration, but Orville was able to fly about 25 feet on May 25. Apparently this was enough to satisfy the media, which paid scant attention to them thereafter. That was fortunate because most of their attempts to fly were just one catastrophe after another.

After months of failures, the brothers conceded they needed a better launching system. They constructed a 25-foot high derrick with a 1600-pound weight which, when released, generated the momentum needed for take-off.

By the middle of September, they were making half-mile flights and turning. Amos Root, a seller of bee-keeping equipment, witnessed a circular flight of 4,080 feet and lasting one minute and 35 seconds. He reported his experience in *Gleanings in Bee Culture*. "When it first turned that circle, and came near the starting point, I was right in front of it, and I said then, and I believe still, it was [

. . .]The grandest sight of my life" (Howard 162). Root offered his article to *Scientific American* but they declined to publish it.

The Wrights already had an audience of local farmers and the crews of the Dayton-Springfield trolley line. In fact, several inspectors held up their trolleys in order to view the flights.

The 1904 flights came to a halt on December 9, almost a full year since their first success. The brothers were very discouraged. In spite of their new launching system, they had not yet developed a reliable airplane suited for practical use.

CHAPTER SEVENTEEN

"FLYER FOR SALE"

In the spring of 1903, Chanute traveled to Europe to stimulate interest in the St. Louis World's Fair. He invited Alberto Santos Dumont, a wealthy Brazilian who flew dirigibles, to exhibit his airship at the 1904 exposition. In Paris he addressed the Aero Club of France. His presentation stimulated French interest in the accomplishments of the Wrights brothers.

Chanute discussed both his own gliding experiments of 1896 and the work of the Wrights in 1902. During his speech, Chanute revealed important information about the Wright's wing warping mechanism, which was the basis of their U.S. patent.

The French enthusiastically received Chanute's speech, but they were appalled to learn that members of another country were more advanced in aeronautics than themselves. A young artillery captain, Louis Ferdinand Ferber, was particularly interested in Chanute's speech. Ferber had been corresponding with Chanute since 1901. He had read about the Wrights' earlier experiments in a German journal and had written Wilbur for additional information.

Another member of the club, Ernest Archdeacon, urged the Aero Club to establish an aviation committee. In order to spur the rapid development of powered flight, Archdeacon suggested offering a prize. Henri Deutsch de la Meurthe, a wealthy oilman, responded, offering a large sum of money for the first airplane flight of one kilometer in a closed circuit. Archdeacon put up a like amount (Howard 187). Those actions sparked a renewed French interest in aviation.

An Englishman, Patrick Y. Alexander, had traveled to Dayton in December 1902. He was a member of the British Aeronautical Society and wanted to meet the only persons who were making any advances in gliding since the death of the English experimenter, engineer Percy Pilcher. Later, when Lieutenant Colonel John Capper, an expert with the British Balloon Factory, traveled to the United States to observe aeronautics in America, Alexander wrote him a letter of introduction to the Wrights.

On October 23, 1904, Colonel Capper came to Dayton. He had already visited the World's Fair and seen William Avery fly one of Chanute's gliders. He stopped in Chicago to see Chanute, the much-respected disseminator of aeronautic information. Then he visited with the Wrights. They showed him photographs of their latest flights. Capper was so impressed with the photographs and with the Wrights that he advised them to submit a proposal to sell the flying machine to the British government when they felt they were ready. In January

1905, the Wrights were ready. They informed Lieutenant Colonel Capper that they were then prepared to submit a proposal.

In February, the British Director of Fortifications and Works sent a letter requesting a proposal. The proposal the Wrights sent in March stated that they could furnish a machine capable of carrying two men fifty miles without refueling. The price was to be based on the distance flown in their longest trial. Howard writes, "If the trial flight covered fifty miles, the price would be a whopping 50,000 pounds or $125,000" (166).

The proposal was referred to the Royal Engineer Committee. The committee felt the machine was too uncertain to make an agreement, but a military attaché was to come to Dayton to observe a flight. He never came.

Even before they had sent a proposal to England, Wilbur had approached a United States Congressman about a possible sale to the American government. This first contact was made on January 3, 1905. Congressman Robert M. Nevin advised Wilbur to write a letter addressed to him and he would personally deliver it to the Secretary of War. When the letter arrived at Congressman Nevin's office, he was ill. An aide forwarded the letter to the Board of Ordnance and Fortification, the same agency that had funded Langley for his $50,000 fiasco. The president of the board replied in a letter to Congressman Nevin on January 25, 1905:

> I have the honor to inform you that, as many requests have been made for financial assistance in the development of designs for flying-machines, the Board has found it necessary to decline to make allotments for the experimental development of devices for mechanical flight, and has determined that, before suggestions with that object in view will be considered, the device must have been brought to the stage of practical operation without the expense to the United States.
>
> It appears from the letter of Messers. Wilbur and Orville Wright that their machine has not yet been brought to the stage of practical operation, but as soon as it shall have been perfected, this Board would be pleased to receive further representations from them in regard to it ("Miracle" 156-157).

The Wrights had been very generous in their proposal. They were not only willing to make machines to the government's specifications, but were willing to turn over all the scientific and practical information they had acquired along with the use of their patent.

The brothers were convinced that war could be prevented with their airplane. They believed neither country would have the advantage because each country would know what the other was doing. Today that view seems naïve, but in 1905 it seemed very logical to them.

The brothers continued to make improvements in their flyer. Their new engine was producing 18 horsepower. But all was not well. The machine continued to have problems. A June 23 trial-flight testing the three control systems ended in an accident. Another catastrophe occurred July 14 when the plane began to wobble at 30 miles per hour. Orville was unable to regain rudder control and the plane crashed, throwing him through the upper wing. He lay bruised and dazed, but he had escaped with his life.

Another test pilot had not been so fortunate. He was Daniel Maloney who had recently died testing a glider for John Joseph Montgomery in California. Maloney's death and Orville's accident highlighted the Wrights' need for caution.

The rainy weather, soggy soil and the exhausting task of laying 60 feet of track, hoisting 1200 pounds of weight to the top of the 25 foot derrick, lifting the 700 pound flyer onto the track before each flight, and carrying it back to the shed at the end of each day's testing severely limited the Wrights' trial time.

But by the end of September the machine was ready for final testing. It was the most visually pleasing of all the Wright machines. It resembled a swan with its long rudder neck looking gracefully forward. On October 5, Wilbur flew the Flyer's longest flight yet - 24 1/5 miles in 38 minutes at a speed of 38 miles per hour (Howard 183).

WILBUR AND ORVILLE WRIGHT AT HUFFMAN PRAIRIE

With the confidence generated from this successful performance, the brothers once again wrote the Secretary of War offering to sell the Wright Flyer. They now proposed to build a machine that would carry one man and fuel for a hundred miles. The price would depend upon the distance covered in its longest trial. The president of the Ordnance Board replied on October 16 and used the very same first paragraph he used in his first letter to the Wrights:

> I have the honor to inform you that, as many requests have been made for financial assistance in the development of designs for flying-machines, the Board has found it necessary to decline to make allotments for the

experimental development of devices for mechanical flight, and has determined that, before suggestions with that object in view will be considered, the device must have been brought to the stage of practical operation without the expense to the United States.

Before the question of making a contract with you for the furnishing of a flying-machine is considered it will be necessary for you to furnish this Board with the approximate cost of the completed machine, the date upon which it would be delivered, and with such drawings and descriptions thereof as are necessary to enable its construction to be understood and a definite conclusion as to its practicability to be arrived at. Upon receipt of this information, the matter will receive the careful consideration of the Board ("Miracle" 149).

The Wrights were sure the Board had misinterpreted their proposal, so they wrote again:

We have no thought of asking financial assistance from the government. We propose to sell the results of experiments finished at our own expense.

In order that we may submit a proposition conforming as nearly as possible to the ideas of your board, it is desirable that we be informed what conditions you would wish to lay down as to the performance of the machine in the official trials, prior to the acceptance of the machine. We cannot well fix a price, or a time for delivery, till we have your idea of the qualifications necessary to such a machine. We ought also to know whether you would wish to reserve a monopoly on the use of the invention, or whether you would permit us to accept orders for similar machines from other governments, and give public exhibitions, etc. Proof of our ability to execute an undertaking of the nature proposed will be furnished whenever desired ("Miracle" 151).

Obviously the Board could not have taken even minimal time to read and process the Wrights' letter. If they had, they never would have replied:

It is recommended that Messrs. Wright be informed that the Board does not care to formulate any requirements for the performance of a flying-machine or take any further action on the subject until a machine is produced which by actual operation is shown to be able to produce horizontal flight and to carry an operator ("Miracle" 152).

The Wrights were understandably dumbfounded. Three times they had offered their machine to the government and three times they were rebuffed. Never was any effort made to investigate their claims. Any member of the board could have picked up the phone and called the Dayton papers. Luther Beard, the editor of the Dayton *Journal,* rode the trolley with the Wrights. On October 5, 1905 the Dayton *Daily News* had run an article about the sensational flights being made at Huffman Prairie. It appears that not one move was made to check out the Wrights' story; thus the government almost let the greatest invention of the new century slip away.

The Wrights were very cautious about whom they allowed to view the flights. They had not been issued a patent, although it had been applied for in early 1904. They were concerned that exhibiting the flying machine would present an opportunity for a would-be inventor to steal their ideas. So, in place of making public demonstrations, they offered the testimony of many respected citizens of the communities where they had flown. Testimony of private citizens is an accepted practice in the court of law, so why shouldn't those seeking to buy the flying machine accept it?

The Wrights needed a buyer, so they started to advertise. In November, Orville wrote Carl Dienstbach, the correspondent of the German journal, one of the first persons to inquire about the Flyer in 1903. In his letter, Orville gives the names of respected citizens who have witnessed the flights; some were in Kitty Hawk and others were in Ohio. Wilbur wrote the French Ambassador, J.J. Jusserand, saying they were considering making a formal proposal to the French government. He invited the ambassador to send an attaché to investigate their claims and even enclosed a note from a leading Dayton citizen who had been present at one of the flights.

Wilbur wrote Chanute and said they had decided to absolve their friends from having to keep secret the results of their experiments. Other letters were written to George Besancon, the editor of the French monthly, *L'Aerophil*, and to their English acquaintance, Patrick Alexander. Alexander presented his letter at the December meeting of the British Aeronautical Society. Carl Dienstbach published his letter in the German journal, *Illustrierte Aeronautische Mitteilungen*. Unfortunately, the editor added some sharp remarks in response to a private letter Captain Ferber had published earlier in which he mistranslated remarks Wilbur had written about the German Kaiser.

In early December 1905, the Wrights received word that all their claims were accepted and they were given a U.S. patent, which would be issued as soon as some minor corrections in the wording were made. This seems to have been the one bright light in the two years since they made the world's first successful powered flight. They had spent the last two years perfecting the machine and building a more powerful engine. Now that they were ready to sell their flyer, no one seemed interested in buying it.

CHAPTER EIGHTEEN

ACROSS THE ATLANTIC

Frank S. Lahm, an American businessman living in Paris, heard about the Wright brothers from members of the Aero Club of France. Lahm was from Mansfield, Ohio, so he asked his brother-in-law, Henry Weaver, Sr., who was living in Ohio, to verify the Wrights' story. Weaver traveled to Dayton in 1905 where he met Orville Wright for the first time. When he first saw him, Orville was sitting in lobby of the Algonquin Hotel holding his hat in his hand, looking tired and drawn. Weaver thought Orville resembled Edgar Allen Poe. The two men found each other quite congenial. They went to Huffman's Prairie to see the flight field and to talk with the local farmers, David Beard and Amos Stauffer. Then, they visited around town interviewing William Founts, the druggist, and several others who had witnessed the Wrights' flights and who were able to verify their claims.

Henry Weaver sent his brother-in-law a glowing report, but when Frank S. Lahm read Weaver's letter at the meeting of the French Aero Club, it created such a stir that President Ernest Archdeacon had to call for order. Most of the members of the club left the meeting convinced that the Wrights had performed a great American bluff.

But Captain Ferber, who had corresponded with both the Wrights and Chanute and had conducted some propeller-driven experiments of his own, wasn't so sure. In May 1905, Ferber had written the Wrights inquiring about the purchase of a Wright Flyer. The Wrights did not reply until October 9, 1905. At that time, they offered the machine for $200,000 (equivalent to one million francs), along with training in its operation. Ferber then informed his superiors that the Wrights were ready to sell their machine for a million francs. Arnold Fordyce represented the French syndicate, which was interested in purchasing the Flyer and presenting it to the French government. He was the secretary to Henri Letellier, whose father owned the influential Paris newspaper, *Le Journal*. An option to buy was arranged and given to the French Minister of War who dispatched a commission to Dayton to discuss the terms with the Wright brothers.

All the negotiations between the Wrights and the commission were kept secret. One of the members of the commission, Commandant Henri Bonel, was a confirmed skeptic. But after he met the Wrights, he was won over by their honesty and sincerity. When he returned to France, he urged the French government to immediately accept the option to buy the Flyer. However, the danger of a war between France and Germany had ended and the French government increased the requirements of the contract. It wanted an exclusive rights period of fifteen months rather than the agreed-upon three months and increased both the speed and altitude requirement. The Wrights refused to change the contract. No agreement was reached and the French government had to pay the contracted forfeiture fee of $5,000. This was the Wrights' first return on their investment. It was not for selling their flying machine, but for not selling it. Although obviously disappointed, they must have enjoyed a good laugh out of that turn of events.

In February, 1906, Albert F. Zahm, a professor of mathematics at Catholic University and an influential member of the Aero Club of America wrote a letter to the Wrights on behalf of Augustus Post, Secretary of the Aero Club of America. In the letter Zahm told the Wrights that the club was adopting a resolution congratulating them on their successful achievement of human flight. At Zahm's recommendation, the brothers prepared a statement describing their aeronautical experiments at Huffman field in 1905. In that document they not only gave a list of the dates, distance and time of their trials but also a list of prominent persons who witnessed those flights. Considering their momentous achievement, they ended the letter with a very modest statement:

> From the beginning the prime object was to devise a machine of practical utility, rather than a useless toy. [. . .] Every effort has been made to increase the scientific efficiency of the wings screws [propellers]. [. . .] The favorable results which have been obtained have been due to improved methods in flying quality and to improved methods of balancing and steering. The motor and machinery possess no extraordinary qualities. The best dividends on the labor invested have invariably come from seeking more knowledge rather than more power" (Jakab and Young 17).

On May 8, 1906, the Wrights sent a letter to the Secretary of the British War Office acknowledging the receipt of an earlier letter and offering the British government "a flyer capable of carrying a man and supplies sufficient for a long trip" (Papers 2: 713). In July, they sent a proposal to Lieutenant Colonel Albert E. Gleichen, the British Military attaché in Washington. Colonel Gleichen came to Dayton in August 1906, apparently to discuss that proposal. However, Lieutenant Colonel Capper, a former British visitor to the Wrights' home, advised his government against making a deal with the Wrights, because he was sure that an experimental glider being developed by John W. Dunne would be the British answer to the Wright Flyer. In fact, he was so confident that he tested the glider himself. He got a rude awakening when he crashed into a Scottish cliff during the first flight of the glider. The glider was destroyed and his face was badly bruised.

After being turned down three times by the U.S. War Department, the Wrights weren't interested in approaching the U.S. government again. So when George Cabot of Boston offered to intervene on their behalf, the Wrights declined his offer.

This appears to have caused some tension between Chanute and Wilbur because in one letter Chanute wrote Wilbur that he [Wilbur] was "too cocksure that theirs is the only secret worth knowing [. . .]" (Howard 202). Wilbur had said."no one will be able to develop a practical flyer within five years." (Howard 202).

Although the Wrights were anxious for a contract, they did not want to rush into just any contract. They wanted to wait until they had a decent offer. Their only exception to this was the American government. They had practically offered to give the Flyer to the War Department, along with all scientific and practical information on the results of their experiments and the use of their patent. They had even asked if the government wished to reserve a monopoly on the use of their machine. They had made the price of the machine contingent on the distance flown in the trial flight

WILBUR AND ORVILLE WRIGHT

But as the machine improved, so did the Wrights' opinion of what it was worth. They did not believe anyone was even near to finding another solution to flying a powered plane. Chanute was not so sure. He had been to Europe and had seen what others were doing.

It was Albert Santos Dumont who proved Chanute right. He won the Aero Club de France award on November 12, 1906. He flew 220 meters. Wilbur conceded that Santo's flight "was the first real indication of progress that [had] been displayed in France in five years" (Howard 205).

On November 30, the Wrights received a visit from a New York businessman who had read about them in the newspaper. Ulysses D. Eddy was a former associate of Flint and Company, a New York firm, which specialized in the promotion and sale of lethal items such as submarines and torpedo boats. Eddy suspected that the flying machine could be used for scouting during a war. He was sure Charles R. Flint, the head of the Flint Company, would be most interested in this new invention. Eddy was immediately captivated with the simplicity of the Hawthorne Street household. He suggested that the brothers consider the possibility of retaining the Flint Company to promote and sell their flying machine. The brothers were definitely interested. Wilbur wrote Chanute saying he and Orville would be meeting with people in New York the following week.

The brothers went to New York where they attended the American Aero Club show with Chanute. During their visit, Ulysses Eddy introduced them to Frank R. Cordley, a member of the Flint firm. Cordley agreed with Eddy's opinion: the firm was interested in promoting the sale of the Flyer. The Wrights were told that a formal agreement would allow the firm to act as their business agent. After having just spent another fruitless year trying to sell their Flyer, the brothers felt this was the help they needed.

On December 12, 1906 Orville returned to New York to discuss the arrangement with the head of the company, Charles Flint. Flint offered the Wrights a half-million dollars for all foreign rights to the Flyer. In January, both Orville and Wilbur returned to New York and another deal was drawn up. The Flints would handle the foreign business but the Wrights wanted to handle the terms and place of the sales. The Flint Company would pay all expenses and receive a 20 per cent commission on all business deals up to a half-million dollars. On anything over that amount, they would receive a 40 per cent commission. That sounded reasonable to the Wrights so they agreed, but they also insisted that no demonstrations would be made until there was a signed contract with the buyer.

When the Wrights were at the Aero Club Show in New York, they met Congressman Herbert Parsons who was the brother-in-law of the club's president. Congressman Parsons intervened on their behalf; he sent President Theodore Roosevelt an article about the Wrights from *Scientific American.* The president forwarded the article to the Secretary of War, William Howard Taft, who then forwarded it to the Board of Ordnance and Fortification. With the endorsement of the president behind this initiative, the Board now felt compelled to take the Wrights' invention seriously. They wrote the Wrights a letter saying that the Board would be glad to hear from them.

The Wrights had already received a telegram from the Flint Company requesting that the Wrights travel to Europe in order to meet with Hart Berg, their agent in charge of marketing in Europe. After much discussion between the brothers, Wilbur agreed to go. Orville planned to go as soon as the new plane and engine were complete. On May 16, 1906, Wilbur was on board the steamship *Campania* on his way to Europe. That left Orville to negotiate the agreement with the United States government. On June 15, 1907, Orville offered the government one machine with instructions for its use for $100,000. The Board wanted exclusive rights. Orville told them this was impossible because of a previous agreement with the Flint Company. The negotiations ended. It seemed the government had closed the door once again.

CHAPTER NINETEEN

A EUROPEAN EXPERIENCE

Hart Berg, the Flint Company agent who worked in Paris, was well aware of the French opinion of the Wrights. But when he first set eyes on Wilbur in London, he was surprised by his own reaction. He wrote to the Flint office in New York, "he was the first person I spoke to, and either I am Sherlock Holmes, or Wright has the peculiar glint of genius in his eye which left no doubt in my mind who he was" (Howard, 217).

Wilbur had assumed he would be gone only a week or two and had packed sparingly. Berg saw how ill-prepared Wilbur was for an extended stay, so he took him to a London tailor and had him fitted for a business suit and dinner jacket. Then Berg and Wilbur spent the rest of the afternoon discussing business in England and France. Wilbur was in favor of approaching the government directly. Berg had to convince him that forming a company, which could make overtures to the government, was a more acceptable way of doing business in Europe. Berg was not quite sure he had convinced Wilbur when he wrote the New York office:

> About 5:00 in the afternoon I think, you will distinctly note that I said 'I think,' I brought about some sort of action in his mind, and think he was on the point, you will note that I say that 'I think he was on the point' of veering around from the government to company methods (Howard 218).

The wealthy oilman who had contributed to the Aero Club of France prize, Henri Deutsch, was interested in forming an international company. He first wanted to approach the Minister of War in order to assess the French government's interest. The minister agreed to entertain a proposal of purchase if the machine could reach an altitude of 300 meters. This had been one of the requirements which had been added to the earlier French contract and which the Wrights had rejected. Wilbur felt they could now reach that altitude, so he agreed to this requirement. The Flint's attorney drew up articles of incorporation. Shares of stock would be offered for sale in France with Deutsch agreeing to buy a large share.

Commandant Bonel, the head of the original commission that had negotiated the first French contract with the Wrights, was overjoyed with this development. He spoke with Arnold Fordyce, who also had been a member of the commission representing the French syndicate, which was to finance the purchase of the Flyer. Bonel thought Fordyce would share his enthusiasm, but apparently he did not. Instead, Fordyce went straight to his employer, Henri

Letellier, head of the syndicate that had originated the first contract with the Wrights. Letellier confronted the War Minister, General George Picquart, who was unaware of the earlier contact with the Wrights. Picquart then told Deutsch the prior arrangement with the aeronautical syndicate was still valid and that all business would be conducted through Letellier. Deutsch was furious; he thought Wilbur and Berg had used him to start the negotiations, so he withdrew his funds. It wasn't until later when Wilbur was able to explain the whole situation to him that their cordial relationship was restored.

Senator Charles Humbert was secretary of the Chamber of Deputies' budget committee, which was responsible for appropriating funds for the purchase of the Flyer. Humbert decided he wanted a piece of the pie, so he added an additional 250,000 francs to the proposal. Wilbur and Berg were appalled at this outright graft and refused to agree to the increase. Humbert was given an ultimatum: put the deal through as it was or no deal They would negotiate with Germany. Humbert told them to return in two days. Three days later they learned the deal was accepted "in principle."

But Berg and Wilbur had already decided they should begin looking elsewhere for a sale. They planned a visit to Germany. With his new clothes still at the London tailor, Wilbur needed to buy some decent clothes to see the German Emperor. He visited a Paris tailor and was fitted for a dress suit and long frock coat. The idea of his brother dressed in formal attire stimulated Orville's funny bone. He wrote, "I would give three cents to see you in your dress suit and plug hat" (Howard 220).

Relations between the brothers weren't always so congenial. With their communications limited to cables and letters flying back and forward over the Atlantic, nerves became frayed. Each became exasperated with the other. Orville complained: "I have practically no information of what is going on. When you cable, you never explain anything so that I can answer with any certainty that we are talking about the same thing" (Papers 2: 793). Wilbur complained he had written and kept nothing back but he asked, "How could I base cables on letters which portrayed a situation entirely different from that existing two weeks earlier?" (Papers 2: 804).

Orville was afraid Wilbur would give away exclusive rights to the French. Wilbur assumed that Orville was spending his time on unimportant things rather than getting the Flyer ready for shipment to Europe. While Wilbur had been busy negotiating the sale of the flying machine, Orville and Charlie Taylor had constructed a new engine, which seemed to be the best they ever built. Then it began having trouble running at high speeds.

Orville had been left the task of redesigning the Flyer to accommodate two men. That meant changing the seating arrangement and revamping the control system. The new system had to have dual controls so that the other person could learn to fly. All of this consumed considerable time.

It is possible that neither brother appreciated what the other was experiencing. They seemed to have worked best when they were together. They had the uncanny ability to know what each other was thinking and were able to complement each other's ideas. The absence of that brotherly support may have added to their crankiness with each other. On July 2, 1907, Wilbur asked Orville,

"When can you come?" The same day he wrote Orville and said that he was hurt because Orville had turned down his recommendations after Orville had given his consent. He complained that he had not received any mail since the middle of June and he didn't know when the machine was coming. Some letters seemed to have been lost *en route* and were never delivered to Wilbur in Paris.

When the work finally was completed on the Flyer, Orville left Dayton to go to Europe on Thursday, July 19, 1907. Wilbur wrote his father a very long letter detailing many of his complaints. It became evident that Wilbur really didn't want to be in Europe negotiating with the French, he wanted to be home working on the new Flyer.

When Orville arrived on Sunday, July 28, at 7:00 a.m., Wilbur was genuinely concerned about Orville's need to recuperate from his ocean voyage. The two brothers seemed to have spent a pleasant day together but got right down to business the next day. They discussed with Cordley and Berg their concern about not having a firm commitment yet.

Later in the day, Arnold Fordyce came to see the brothers to get their revised proposal. He confused the situation by translating the proposal into French, stating what they wouldn't do rather than what they would do. Then Fordyce took the proposal to the French government, which then insisted on exclusive rights for a full year. Berg told Fordyce to go back and make sure the rest of the contract was satisfactory before they negotiated further.

Berg and Wilbur went to Germany on August 4, 1907, and left Orville in Paris to try to work out a deal with the French government. Orville was subjected to the same type of intrigue as Wilbur had been earlier. Senator Humbert had not given up. Now he tried to persuade Major A. L. Targe that the Wrights were frauds.

Wilbur was initially poorly received in Germany because the editor of *L'Aerophile* had mistranslated a remark written by Wilbur in a private letter to Ferber. What Wilbur wrote was: "With Russia and Austria-Hungry in their present troubled condition and the German Emperor in a truculent mood, a spark may produce an explosion at any time" ("Miracle" 170). The editor had translated "in a truculent mood" to mean seeking a quarrel. However, after Wilbur met with the members of the newly formed German aeronautical program and other industrial leaders, he was invited to submit a proposal to the German government. He hammered out a proposal in which he would offer a machine for 100,000 marks and 50,000 marks to train a pilot, but he did not offer exclusive rights even for a short period and would never again.

Wilbur did not offer the proposal to the Germans at that time; he felt he needed to wait until he knew the state of affairs in France. He returned to France to determine the status of negotiations. It was still chaotic. No agreement had been reached.

The Wrights then decided to offer the French the same contract they hoped to offer the Germans. They translated the new proposal into French and then asked Fordyce to present it to the Minister of War. Fordyce made all kinds of excuses saying it was in poor form, it was a bad translation, etc. At that time the Wrights concluded the French were acting in bad faith and withdrew their offer.

Wilbur returned to Germany, but found the Germans were unwilling to sign a contract until they saw the machine fly. Wilbur felt tempted to comply but decided it was too late in the fall season.

All negotiations seemed dead, but their European time hadn't been a total loss. While in Paris, they had been invited to visit with Frank Lahm. His son, a U.S. lieutenant in Paris attending a French Cavalry school, met the Wrights at his father's home. Lieutenant Frank Lahm was recalled to the United States to take command of the aeronautical section of the U.S. Signal Corps. After meeting the Wrights, he wrote to the highest officer on the Army Board telling him of an interview he recently had with Mr. Orville Wright of Dayton, Ohio. Lieutenant Lahm relayed information about the success of the Wright Flyer, which had been invented by two brothers from his home state of Ohio, Orville and Wilbur Wright. He expressed the opinion that this invention had military value and would be most useful in the event of war. He stated that he thought it unfortunate that the aeroplane be purchased by other countries before the United States acquired it.
In October, the Board of Ordnance and Fortification sent a letter requesting the Wrights to meet with them. Orville replied that they would be happy "to furnish the first machine" to their own government.

With all European negotiations at a standstill, Wilbur returned to America aboard the *H.M.S. Baltic.* Orville remained behind to arrange for the manufacture of engines for the five planes under construction in Dayton. The brothers planned to return to Europe in the spring, hoping their demonstrations would land a buyer.

After conferring with Cordley at the Flint office, Wilbur went to Washington to meet with three high-ranking Army officers. Wilbur offered the Wright Flyer for $25,000. But it was the end of the year and the Army only had $10,000 left in its budget. It seemed as if this sale was lost, too. But this time the Army was serious; it retrieved the remaining funds from the Spanish-American War. On December 23, the Army advertised for bids for a heavier-than-air flying machine. The machine would be required to have seating for a pilot and passenger, be able to fly 125 miles at a speed of 40 hours per hour and remain aloft for the space of an hour. It also had to be portable.

The year, 1907, ended with the first real possibility of a sale. But what happened next is hard to believe!

CHAPTER TWENTY

NOT ONE, BUT TWO

The Wrights submitted their proposal to the United States Signal Corps on January 27, 1908. It was accompanied by the ten per cent forfeiture check, which was required by the bid regulations. If they failed to meet the terms stated in the contract, they would forfeit $2,500.

The plane the Wrights proposed to build was to weigh about 1,250 pounds, seat two men, and be capable of traveling at a speed of 40 miles per hour for the duration of an hour. It would have a water-cooled gasoline engine. The delivery date was to be within two hundred days.

They included a photograph of the 1905 flying machine along with drawings and the request that these be kept confidential.

The Signal Corps had hoped to avoid controversy by advertising for bids, but this was not to be. The government agency was taken to task by several prominent newspapers. The *New York Globe* commented, "no such machine has ever been constructed." *The American Magazine of Aeronautics* proclaimed, "There is not a known flying machine in the world which could fulfill these requirements" (Howard 231). James Mean, editor of the *Aeronautical Annual,* was more fanciful in his denunciation. He wrote Chanute, "I believe that Minerva came forth fully fledged from the head of Jupiter, but I hardly think the perfect flying machine will appear in such a sudden fashion" (Howard 231).

If the Signal Corps thought it would receive only one bid, it was badly mistaken. Apparently many Americans had been very busy trying to find a solution to the problem of flight. The Signal Corps received forty-one bids, but only three of the bidders included the ten per cent certified check with their proposal. The lowest bidder, J.F. Scott of Chicago, eventually withdrew his bid.

That left the Wrights and one other bidder, who turned out to be none other than their old camp companion, Augustus Herring. Herring had more brass than a brass band. In 1903 when the Wrights had successfully made the first powered flight, he claimed to have independently solved the problem of powered flight and suggested that he and the Wrights form a partnership in which he would get a third of the profits (Papers 1: 213).

Herring's bid of $20,000 under-bid the Wrights by $5,000. The Signal Corps had the good sense to accept both bids. After all, the bidder had to demonstrate his claim by giving demonstrations of the machine's capabilities. If both machines gave satisfactory performances, they would just have to find another $20,000.

Evidently the Wrights weren't the least bit concerned about Herring's bid. After all, they knew the flimsy job he did of building Chanute's gliders and they knew he lacked skill as a flyer. But they suspected that he would once again approach them to build his machine on commission. They couldn't have been more right. He did indeed request that they build his machine.

When the Wrights refused, the charade was up. Herring needed either to produce a powered machine or to withdraw his bid. He couldn't quite bring himself to withdraw, so he asked for an extension. When he finally arrived in Washington with his assistant, they brought two suitcases and a trunk. Somewhere inside that luggage was his plane.

But by the spring of 1909 Herring was up to his old tricks again and spread the rumor that he had already completed his trials in private. He then withdrew his proposal, stating that he had a more desirable offer from a "foreign syndicate," which was none other than Glenn Curtis.

In 1908 Glenn Curtiss was associated with a group of young aeronautics enthusiasts headed by Alexander Graham Bell, the inventor of the telephone. Bell had become interested in aeronautics through his friendship with Langley of Aerodrome fame. This industrious group proposed to accomplish in six months what it had taken the Wrights five years to achieve. Besides Curtis and Bell, there were two Canadians, John A. D. (Douglas) McCurdy and Fredrick W. (Casey) Baldwin, and an American Signal Corps Officer, Lieutenant Tom Selfridge.

The Aerial Experiment Association or AEA was Bell's answer to the Wright brothers. The young men of the AEA would do his experimenting. All were college graduates except Curtis; he was a motorcycle racer and builder of motors. He was a gifted mechanic who added greatly to the practical application of Bell's theories.

Bell built a gigantic man-carrying kite, the Frost King, and he needed a motor. He commissioned Curtis to build him one. Curtis delivered it to Bell's estate at Bein Breagh in Nova Scotia and was invited to join the group as chief engineer. "Bell Boys," as they came to be called, were enthralled by experimenting with a Herring-Chanute type glider built at the Curtis plant. After their first gliding experience, they became extremely interested in powered airplane flight.

Curtiss wrote the Wrights telling them of his newly acquired interest in aeronautics and offering them a motor "gratis." Lieutenant Selfridge also wrote the Wrights asking for specific information. On January 18, 1908, the Wrights answered Selfridge's letter, replying that the information he was seeking was contained in Wilbur's speeches before the Western Society of Engineers which were published in the journals of the Society in December 1901 and August 1903, in Chanute's article in the *Revue des Sciences* published in 1903, and in their U.S. patent 821,393. The Wrights later claimed that in that letter, they gave Selfridge the information he used to develop the ailerons, which were used on the AEA's plane, *White Wing*.

In 1908, the *Scientific American* offered a trophy for a straightway-powered flight of one kilometer in the hopes of luring the Wrights. The Wrights were preoccupied with preparing for the trial demonstrations to secure the Army contract and were not interested in expending their energies competing for a trophy. So, they declined the invitation to fly in the competition.

Meanwhile the French had been very busy trying to catch up to the Wrights. They had been unnerved by Chanute's talk to the Aero Club of France in 1903. His speech offended French pride and a flurry of aeronautical activity followed.

Louis Bleriot had designed a tandem-winged plane similar to Langley's Aerodrome. He flew and crashed it in April, 1907. He tried again in September and December. Both times he crashed his planes. Chanute wrote, "Bleroit built and crashed more machines than any aviator in the world" (Howard 233).

Leon Delagrange, a Parisian sculptor, flew a plane built by Charles and Gabriel Voisin. He bettered the record of Santos in his 14-Ibis. Delagrange flew 40 seconds on November 9, 1907.

Two days later, Henri Farman, an auto racer, flew a 74 second flight. He was invited to do a four-city tour in the United States. After only getting ten feet off the ground for 40 seconds, his tour was canceled.

With all these promising developments taking place in France, it is amazing that Hart Berg was able to put together a private syndicate for the manufacture and sale of the Wright Flyer. Deutsch de La Meurthe was a large stockholder, but none of Letellier's acquaintances were included. A prominent Parisian businessman, Lazare Weiller, was to head the syndicate. Thus La Compaignie Generale de Navigation Aerienne became the French Wright company. The Wrights received stock, royalties on all machines sold and cash for demonstrations made in France. On March 15, 1908, Wilbur went to New York to discuss the details with Flint and Company.

The brothers then faced a new problem. They had two contracts, each requiring demonstration flights, but they hadn't flown since October 1905. In the one and a half years since their last flight, their time had been consumed by improving the engine, which was now 35 horsepower, constructing parts for new planes, writing numerous letters and stumping across Europe trying to drum up a sale.

Now with two contracts on hand, they had no time to waste. They would have to redesign the Flyer to accommodate a passenger who was also learning to fly. That meant rearranging the control system so it could be operated from either seat.

They needed a place that offered few interruptions. That wasn't Huffman Prairie. They needed someplace more secluded. That meant the Outer Banks of North Carolina.

CHAPTER TWENTY-ONE

A SECLUDED PLACE

On Monday, April 6, 1908, Wilbur was on his way to Kitty Hawk, North Carolina. When he arrived in Norfolk, he found that his trunk had been lost in transit. Nevertheless he proceeded on to Elizabeth City. When he arrived at the Elizabeth City depot, he met Captain Daniels, who had assisted during the first flight. Daniels reported that their buildings had been badly damaged in a severe storm just after Christmas. In fact, one was missing all together. The other had lost its roof and one whole side. And to make matters worse, vacationing boys had carried off whatever they could. The lifesavers had salvaged the pump and were using it at the lifesaving station.

Captain Franklin Midgett's schooner didn't arrive in Elizabeth City for two days. When the *Lou Willis* did arrived, it was not the captain but his son, "Little" Spencer, who was sailing it. Meanwhile, Wilbur checked into the Southern Hotel, but he probably didn't sleep much because of all the fires in town that night. When the *Lou Willis* arrived, it was loaded with the supplies and lumber Wilbur had purchased. Thankfully, Captain Franklin Midgett had also come in his new gasoline launch and Wilbur crossed Albemarle Sound in relative comfort.

Wilbur's first sight of the camp must have been heartrending. The new building had been blown away and the hangar was a shell of its former self. Just when time was of the essence, valuable time would be lost rebuilding. Wilbur had no place to stay; even the water pump was gone.

He would have to rely on the hospitality of the Kill Devil Hills lifesavers. He wrote his father that they were very friendly. On April 9 Wilbur wrote Orville describing the ghastly situation. Getting the lumber to the old site would be laborious, but setting up a new location closer to the sound would be disastrous as well. Wilbur said the "best place would be near the old fish landing but the bugs that bite would probably eat us up before we fairly got to experimenting, so I think now that I will go down near the old place again. [. . .] I will expect you with relief Saturday. I am not sure I can hold out much longer" ("Miracle" 258).

Wilbur was frustrated with the delays; little did he know that more delays were coming. The rest of the lumber, which was to be brought in on the *Lou Willis*, was on its way back to Elizabeth City. The boat had been caught in gale force winds and her sails torn off. She returned to port to have them repaired.

But even in the mist of all his troubles, the beauty of the Outer Banks seduced Wilbur. He wrote in his diary, "The evening was beautiful, the moon was almost full." If Wilbur had see the moon reflecting off the ocean, he was privileged to see one of the most breathe-taking sights in the world. It rivaled any of the famous pictures he had seen in the Louvre.

After hiring two Outer Bankers on April 13, Wilbur started rebuilding the living quarters. It was then that he discovered only half the lumber needed for the foundation had been delivered. So, they started working on the hangar roof, which also had been blown off in the storm. While he was at the lifesaving station waiting for the needed lumber, he spied a man hanging around the campsite. Thinking it was one of the two men he had hired, he approached the camp and discovered it was Charlie Furman, a mechanic from Dayton who was interested in flight. Charlie, too, would have to stay with the lifesavers.

No one should ever have to have a birthday like Wilbur did that year. It rained all day, and the wind blew so hard it was impossible to unload the lumber from the *Lou Willis*, which had arrived the previous night.

Just when it seemed things couldn't get any worst, the next day Wilbur came down with diarrhea and the high winds blew so much water out of the sound that the *Lou Willis* was grounded. Charlie Furman found some men to move the lumber to a flat bottom boat, which was towed by gasoline launch to the camp. But when all the lumber was unloaded, Wilbur found that the siding and sheeting were missing.

It wasn't until April 18 that all of the lumber finally arrived at the campsite. Then pouring rain caused an early termination to the rebuilding, and Wilbur returned to the station to rest. He still had diarrhea.

Much hard work must have ensued between that day and the day Orville arrived on April 25. Other than cleaning up trash, the buildings were ready for habitation. Their first night together, the three men slept very soundly - Wilbur in his hanging cot, Orville on some boards thrown across the rafters and Charlie on the floor.

Although the rain and high winds continued for several more days, it no longer disturbed the Wrights. They could work inside the hangar to assemble the modified Flyer.

Word leaked out, probably via the telegraph, that the Wrights were back experimenting on the Outer Banks. The Norfolk *Virginian-Pilot* ran another fanciful tale about a ten-mile flight out to sea and back. News services spread the story.

The New York *Herald* dispatched Bruce Salley to get the "real" story. Salley walked boldly into camp and asked what was going on. The Wrights weren't interested in giving him any information, so he left.

Salley couldn't have foreseen that the very next day, May 6, Orville would make his first flight in one and a half years. Salley had stayed in Manteo that day. But the ever-obliging lifesavers telephoned the details of the flight to him. When his story was published, it ignited so much public interest in the Wright's experiments that the major newspapers dispatched their best reporters to get eyewitness accounts of the happenings on the sand dunes of Kill Devil Hills. These turn-of-the-century reporters bore hardships today's reporters can only imagine: a bone-jarring train ride to Elizabeth city, a sea-sickening voyage across the Albemarle Sound, a sleepless night in a southern inn and bad food. But that was only the beginning; they had to rise by 4:00 a.m. and travel by gasoline launch to a spot across from the Wright's camp. Then they had to crawl over fallen trees; were scratched by thorny vines and brambles; were bitten by mosquitoes, ticks and deer flies; scared silly by the thought of poisonous snakes and spiders; and were frightened by the sudden movement of wild hogs and deer. All for a story. But their heroic efforts were rewarded. They were the first reporters ever to witness the "miracle" of human flight.

JOUNALISTS SPYING ON THE WRIGHT BROTHERS, 1908

Byron Newton wrote in his account in the New York *Herald*:
> The machine rose obliquely into the air. At first it came directly toward us, so that we could not tell how fast it was going, except that it appeared to increase in size as it approached. In the excitement of this first flight, men trained to observe details under all sorts of distractions, forgot their cameras, forgot their watches, forgot everything but this aerial monster chattering over our heads. As it neared us we could plainly see the operator in his seat working the upright levers close by his side. When it was almost squarely over us there was a movement of the forward and rear guiding planes [wings], a slight curving of the large planes at one end and the machine wheeled at an angle every bit as gracefully as an eagle flying close to the ground could have done (Crouch 357).

The reporters saw three flights that day. One was 2,750 yards, flown by Orville. James Hare took the first photograph ever published of the Wright Flyer. It appeared in the May 30,1908 issue of *Collier's Magazine* accompanied by a story by Arthur Ruhl, a freelance writer.

The members of the Kill Devil Hills lifesaving station were the news broadcasters of the Outer Banks. They kept the Wrights informed of the movements of the reporters and they informed the reporters of the activities at the Wright camp.

The Wrights had no time for the reporters' antics. They were racing against time. They needed all the practice they could get to be ready for their contract demonstration trials.

Harry Harper, a London journalist, wrote about the noise of the motor:

One did not hear much of them. What one did hear quite clearly was an odd sort of chattering, clattering sound from the crossed chains, which drove the two long-bladed airscrews. And there was also a penetrating whistling sound from the air-screws themselves. The net result was a mingled whistling, chattering hum which, once heard, could never be forgotten (Howard 245).

At 8:00 a.m. on May 14, Orville flew the first passenger flight. Charlie Furman was the lucky man. His flight lasted 3 minutes and 40 seconds.

Wilbur seemed to have more trouble than Orville working the new control system. On the day of the first passenger flights, Wilbur made a seven and a half minute flight, which ended abruptly. The newspaper reporters had left for the day thinking the flights had ended. They were right; that day was the end of the flights.

The plane was in shambles. Wilbur had pushed the elevator forward instead of backward and the plane crashed while it was flying 50 miles per hour. Orville had been watching through a spyglass. When his brother didn't reappear immediately, Orville and Charlie rushed to the site. They found a dazed Wilbur checking the damage.

The absent reporters learned about the crash as soon as they arrived at Manteo's Tranquil House Inn. Their stories appeared in the leading newspapers the next day. They used their vivid imaginations to supply the missing details. Their lively tales ended with Wilbur in despair over the loss of his only airplane.

The Flint Company officials had repeatedly telegraphed the Wrights during the previous two weeks that one of them was needed immediately in France before the new syndicate collapsed even as it was getting organized. Wilbur would have to go directly from North Carolina to New York before leaving for Europe. Katharine could pack his clothes and send them to him there. Orville would have to complete the machine for the Army trials. On April 19, 1908 Wilbur left the Outer Banks for the last time. He would never again return to this spit of sand jutting out into the waters of the Atlantic, but he could fly now, because of the time spent experimenting on the sandy shores of the North Carolina coast.

CHAPTER TWENTY-TWO

MORE DELAYS

Wilbur worried little about the clothes Katharine would pack for his trip to France. He knew he could depend upon her; she was always there for him, encouraging him, cajoling him, just like the schoolteacher she was.

But this time things were a little different. Apparently knowing that Wilbur needed his clothes immediately, Katharine had packed them in such a hurry that she didn't even open his hatbox and check inside.

Wilbur was wearing Orville's old green work cap when he departed from North Carolina. In New York City, he wanted to wear something more presentable. When he opened the hatbox, he found it was totally empty! His little green work cap became his trademark in France and even set a fashion trend there. Everyone wanted a "Vreecht cap" (Howard 283).

Wilbur had hoped to write an article identifying the unique features of the Wright Flyer. He was concerned that people would begin to think of these features in connection with other planes such as Bell's Boys' *White Wing*. But his presence was needed to bolster the proposed French syndicate. Since he was unable to write the article himself, he asked Orville to write it. While he was sailing across the Atlantic Ocean toward France, he wrote Orville detailed instructions about what the article should cover.

By the time the letter reached Dayton, Orville had already written and mailed the article to *Century Magazine*. "The Wright Brothers Aeroplane" appeared in the September 1908 issue of *Century* and contained only one reference to the material Wilbur had wanted published. It mentioned that "movable rudders working in conjunction with the twisting of the wings" were a part of the Wright patent. Howard calls the article "the first authentic popular account of the invention of the airplane" (Howard 252).

In his article Orville described for his readers what it was like to ride in an early plane. He wrote:

> In order to show the general reader the way in which the machine operates, let us fancy ourselves ready for the start. The machine is placed upon a single rail track facing the wind, and is securely fastened with a cable. The engine is put in motion, and the propellers in the rear whir. You take your seat at the center of the machine beside the operator. He slips the cable, and you shoot forward. An assistant, who has been holding the machine in balance on the rail, starts forward with you, but before you have gone fifty feet the speed is too great for him, and he lets go. Before reaching the end of the track the operator moves the front rudder, and the

machine lifts from the rail like a kite supported by the pressure of the air underneath it. The ground under you is at first a perfect blur, but as you rise the objects become clearer. At a height of one hundred feet you feel hardly any motion at all, except for the wind that strikes your face. If you did not take the precaution to fasten your hat before starting, you have probably lost it by this time. The operator moves a lever: the right wing rises, and the machine swings about to the left. You make a very short turn, yet you do not feel the sensation of being thrown from your seat, so often experienced in automobile and railway travel. You find yourself facing toward the point from which you started. The objects on the ground now seem to be moving at much higher speed, though you perceive no change in the pressure of the wind on your face. You know then that you are traveling with the wind. When you near the starting-point, the operator stops the motor while still high in the air. The machine coasts down at an oblique angle to the ground, and after sliding fifty feet or a hundred feet comes to a rest. Although the machine often lands when traveling at a speed of a mile a minute, you feel no shock whatever, and cannot, in fact, tell the exact moment at which it first touched the ground. The motor close beside you kept up an almost deafening roar during the whole flight, yet in your excitement, you did not notice it till it stopped! (Jakab and Young 32).

Not only did Orville write the *Century Magazine* article, but also he wrote a letter describing the 1908 Kitty Hawk experiences, and sent copies to *Scientific American, Aeronautics, L'Aerophile, Mitteilugen,* and the Aero Club of America. (Crouch 362).

Before Wilbur had boarded the *Touraine* for Europe, he wrote to Orville that he was concerned Orville would attempt to do too much and fail. The letter contained the prophetic statement, "It always takes more time to do things than is expected." Another worry of his was their "approaching financial stringency" (Papers 2: 883).

On his way home from the Outer Banks, Orville had stopped in Washington, D.C., to inspect the parade grounds at Fort Myer, which were to be used in the Wrights trial demonstrations. Orville was left with the bulk of the work. He had to prepare machines for the American trials and begin to construct the airplanes that might be needed for possible sales. Then there was the matter of the engine, which was damaged in Wilbur's last flight; it had to be repaired.

Both brothers wrote each other on June 3, 1908. Wilbur wanted to know why he hadn't received a letter from Orville. He even went so far as to say if Orville had mailed anything from Elizabeth City, Norfolk, Washington or even when Orville had arrived home, he would have received it already. Wilbur was sure that Orville had not stopped in Washington to look at the parade grounds because the papers had not mentioned it. But Wilbur was in for a surprise. Orville's letter told him everything Wilbur had asked about in his own letter and much more.

During his stay in Washington, Orville discussed the wording of their contract with Lieutenant Lahm. Before he left, he received news that the word "time" would be changed to "speed" as the brothers had requested. He had also learned they would have eight-to-ten men to assist them and that the army was anxious for the demonstration trials to begin.

By the time Orville wrote his letter on June 3, he had inventoried the engine building supplies, had cut up all the lumber on hand for front framing and spars, written the article and letters mentioned above and reconstructed the Kitty Hawk flights so he could send Wilbur a map. With his letter he enclosed the map and the distance of each of their flights. Orville also wrote Wilbur on June 7 and again on June 8. Those long descriptive letters should have relieved Wilbur of any concerns about what was happening on the home front; he had enough troubles of his own in France.

The French firm of Bariquand and Marre, to whom Orville had given the instructions and drawings for building the Wrights engines, had not completed a single engine by the time Wilbur arrived back in France. The model engine the Wrights had left them wasn't even assembled. Wilbur was furious. He had to return again and again to the factory. When he finally got his old engine back, they had damaged it so much trying it get it started that Wilbur had to spend days fixing it.

The one thing Wilbur did seem to enjoy was his rides into the countryside in search of a suitable demonstration site. He decided on the racecourse at Le Mans. It was a hundred miles from Paris and near Leon Bollee's automobile factory. Bollee had offered Wilbur a workspace and a team of mechanics to help him.

But Wilbur's troubles were far from over. When he opened the crates containing the Flyer that had been stored at the custom's shed in Havre, he was shocked. Ribs were broken, the muslin torn, the radiators smashed, the axles and tubes of the propellers mashed and bent. As usual Wilbur took out his frustration on Orville. He said in his letter, "I am sure that with a scoop shovel I could have put things in within two or three minutes and made fully as good a job of it. I never saw such evidence of idiocy in my life" (Papers 2: 900). Orville knew that Wilbur was stressed, so he didn't press the matter, but later he did comment on it.

It took Wilbur six weeks to get the Flyer ready. He had planned on only three weeks to prepare. His fingers were raw from pulling the shrunken muslin taut so it could be sewed. The French mechanic didn't know English and Wilbur didn't know much French. Since the man couldn't understand what Wilbur wanted, Wilbur did all the work himself.

Finally, on June 24, Wilbur received the motor Bariquand and Marre had shipped to the Bollee factory. He still had to work on it. On July 4, while he was adjusting the motor, the radiator hose popped off, scalding him with boiling water. Leon Bollee, who was standing behind, him helped Wilbur to the floor. Then Bollee applied picric acid to his burns. Wilbur had a foot long burn on his forearm and a burn the size of his fist on his side. The pain and frustration of this latest delay did nothing to soothe Wilbur's temper. Once again Orville became his whipping boy. On July 9 Wilbur wrote:

> If you had permitted me to have any anticipation of the state in which you had shipped things over here, it would have saved three weeks' time probably. I would have made preparations to build a machine instead of

trying to get along with no assistance and no tools. If you have any conscience it ought to be pretty sore. [. . .]("Miracle" 283).

His letter to Orville contrasted sharply with his letters to his father and sister. In his father's letter he said, "I have had a little trouble [. . .] recently." If in his father's letter he downplayed the severity of his accident, in Katharine's letter he joked about it. Then he ended with this advice: "If you ever get burned do not waste money on doctors, but get a barrel of oil and fill up your bath tub and crawl in and stay till you are well" ("Miracle" 282).

On the very same day that Wilbur scalded himself, Glenn Curtiss won the Scientific American trophy by flying 5,360 feet in a minute and 40 seconds. When the papers reported that the machine would sell for $5,000, Orville wrote Curtis reminding him that, although they had given the AEA information, they had not given them "permission to use the patented features of our machines for exhibitions or in a commercial way" (Papers 2:907). This letter was just a foretaste of the conflict over the patent infringements, which would eventually end in court. Orville had declined to enter that race citing lack of time due to preparing for the Army demonstration trials, which were scheduled for the fall.

CHAPTER TWENTY-THREE

IN FULL VIEW

Wilbur's burns took over a month to heal, but he was determined to resume flying. Under cover of darkness, he and his new friend, Leon Bollee, mounted the Flyer on a two-wheeled cart and towed it behind Bollee's automobile to the Les Hunaudieres racecourse near Le Mans. A small wooden shed became home to Wilbur and the Flyer. He had a stove for cooking and was supplied with canned goods from M. Pellier, manufacturer of fine French canned goods. A small restaurant was near by, as was a farmhouse where he purchased his water, milk and ice. The weather cleared on August 8, 1908, Wilbur decided to "do a little something." Fred Howard writes:

> the "little something" that Wilbur did on August 8,1908, can best be compared to the first American landing on the moon on July 20, 1969, for the world was ushered into the air age that Saturday at the little country racetrack near Le Mans just as surely as it was ushered into the age of space sixty-one years later by Neil Armstrong's first feathery footsteps on the surface of the moon (Howard 255).

The casual crowd that had assembled with their boater hats and picnic baskets were in for a thrill of a lifetime. Eighty feet of track were laid; the derrick stood poised with 1500 pounds of cast-iron disks waiting to be released from its apex.

The Flyer was moved out of the shed and hauled to the track. The crowd waited in anticipation, but Wilbur would not be rushed. He waited until it was perfectly calm. At 6:30 p.m., the engine sputtered to life, the propellers whirled; Wilbur reversed his green cap and climbed into the seat located on the lower wing. The weights were released, the Flyer moved forward gradually, and then it accelerated and rose majestically into the evening twilight. The crowd was breathless, a spontaneous cheer rose from the grandstand. Then a gasp and a scream arose from the crowd. Wilbur was headed straight for a stand of poplar trees at the end of the track. Finally, Wilbur did what no French aviator could do at the time, he banked, turned sharply and flew down the other side of the track. It was no bluff; the Wrights could fly! It only took one minute and forty-five seconds to transform the doubting Frenchmen into believers.

WILBUR WRIGHT AT LE MANS, 1908

The French aviators who were present were overwhelmed. George Besancon spoke for the French aviators in *L'Aerophile.*

> The facility with which the machine flies, and the dexterity with which the aviator gave proof from the first, in his maneuvering, have completely dissipated all doubts. Not one of the former detractors of the Wrights dare question, today, the previous experiments of the men who were truly the first to fly [. . .] (Crouch 368).

The French newspaper *Le Figaro:*

I've seen him; I've seen them! Yes! I have seen today Wilbur Wright and his great white bird, the beautiful mechanical bird. [. . .] There is no doubt! Wilbur and Orville Wright have well and truly flown" (Crouch 368).

But Charles and Gabriel Voissin, builders of French flying machines, still had to grumble a little. They sent a joint letter to *Le Matin.*

Where was aviation born? They asked. "IN FRANCE" Without wishing to diminish at all the merit of the aviators of Dayton, we permit ourselves to make the observation that French aviation was not born uniquely by their experiments; and that if we have derived some information - moreover very little - from their tests, they have also profited from French genius in large measure (Crouch 369).

But even this expression of envy couldn't detract from the impact of the flights at Le Mans. Wilbur continued to thrill the crowds. On Monday he completed two circuits of the track doing figure-eights before a crowd of 2,000. On Tuesday before a crowd of 3,000, he flew three circuits of the field and rose to an altitude of seventy feet. The crowd was spellbound.

But on Thursday, after seven circuits of the field and eight minutes of airtime, he made a tight circle, lost power and was forced to land. The impact of the abrupt landing caused the left wing to smash into the ground. Wilbur emerged unharmed. The crowd went wild! Wilbur Wright, in less than a week, had become their hero, "as superb in his accidents as in his flights."

Now that Wilbur had captured the heart of France, the French Army agreed to let him use the artillery range at Camp d'Auvours. It was a more suitable field and one which Wilbur had preferred in the first place. The Flyer was moved once again with the aid of Bollee's automobile.

That very same day Orville boarded the train for Washington, D.C., to prepare for the U.S. Army trials. Orville wrote Wilbur on August 23, 1908, from the Army base at Fort Myer. It was a very positive letter. He was satisfied with the field, although it was small and he didn't anticipate any trouble if he got enough practice. He ended the letter with a little dig: "the goods came through in perfect shape. They were packed exactly as were the goods sent to Europe" ("Miracle" 296).

When the engine arrived at Fort Myer, there were several days of adjustments, after which the Signal Corps log reported on August 31, "Engine being run to ease" (Papers 2: 917). Several minor mishaps took place; the dolly jumped the track causing the Flyer to topple to the ground, but no damage was done. On the same day, Lieutenant Creecy, USMC, was busy untwisting the derrick ropes when 400 pounds of cast-iron disks descended on his chin. He surely had a very sore jaw for several days, but no mention is made of it in the Signal Corps log.

The log notes that the first flight was one minute, eleven seconds at a speed of thirty-five miles an hour. The Flyer's right side front skid was broken in two places; the water hose jarred loose and the radiator needed more screws. That first flight electrified the small crowd of less than a thousand spectators. One admiring observer was Theodore Roosevelt, Jr., President Teddy Roosevelt's son. He described what happened when the Flyer became airborne: "The crowd's gasp of astonishment was not alone at the wonder of it, but because it was so unexpected. I'll never forget the impression the sound from the crowd made on me. It was the sound of complete surprise" (Kelly 227).

When Orville landed in a cloud of dust, newsmen rushed forward, some with tears streaming down their cheeks, overwhelmed by having seen what they considered the impossible. But if the reporters were impressed, apparently the newspaper editors were not, because even in Washington the story was relegated to an inside page.

On September 9, Orville had breakfast with Augustus Post, Secretary of the Aero Club of America. About nine o'clock, Orville climbed on board the Flyer and began circling the field. Each time the Flyer completed a circle around the parade ground, Augustus Post made a tally mark on an envelope. Fifty-seven marks later Orville landed. He had been in the air 57 1/2 minutes and had just set the world record for endurance. That day the Signal Corps log noted, "Today's flight was the world's record up to date for a gasless heavier-than-air machine" (Papers 2: 921). Word reached official Washington. Desktops slammed closed; offices were locked. Bodies swarmed across the Potomac. At 5:19, Orville turned on the engine, the propellers began whirring. The weights were lowered, the Flyer moved forward, slowly at first, but as it accelerated, it lifted from the track and became airborne. Orville's circuits over the parade ground were much wider this time. He completed fifty-five circles, his air time was sixty-two minutes and fifteen seconds. In one short hour, Orville had captivated official Washington which included the secretaries of War, the Navy, Commerce and Labor.

When most of the crowd had departed, Orville invited his friend, Lieutenant Frank Lahm, to sit beside him in the Flyer's passenger seat. It was Lieutenant Lahm who had persuaded the War Department to reconsider purchasing the Flyer. Just as daylight was fading and the moon was beginning to rise, the Flyer ascended into the misty twilight sky. The ride lasted six minutes, twenty-four seconds. It was a new world record for a two-man flight.

On Thursday, Orville set a 200-foot world altitude record and on Friday he set a new endurance record of one hour and eleven minutes. Octave Chanute was one of the spectators. Then on Saturday he broke his own endurance record and flew one hour and fourteen minutes. He set another passenger record when he took Major Squier of the Aeronautical Board for a nine-minute ride.

Monday, Tuesday and Wednesday of the following week, the Flyer was land-bound due to high winds. By Thursday the weather was suitable for flight. Lieutenant Selfridge, the secretary of the AEA who had requested information on flight from the Wrights, asked for a ride. Orville felt very uneasy about this, but since he had given the other officers rides, he felt obliged to honor Selfridge's request.

At five o'clock on September 17, 1908, Orville and Lieutenant Selfridge boarded the Flyer. Orville circled the field three times then eased the Flyer up to an altitude of one hundred feet. Suddenly, he heard a soft tapping in the rear of the machine. He turned around but saw nothing that indicated that there was a problem; however, he decided to turn off the power as soon as he could turn the plane around. Then he heard two loud thumps and the plane shook violently.

Immediately, Orville turned off the engine and turned the plane around, but the Flyer headed downward.

The plane hit the ground with such force that both men were severely injured and the Flyer was wrecked. Selfridge had hit his head on one of the wooden uprights. The blow fractured his skull. When Orville was pulled from the wreckage, he was still conscious and asked about Selfridge. Both men were transported to the base hospital on stretchers. Selfridge was rushed immediately into surgery. He died five minutes after coming out of the operating room. Orville was more fortunate. It was thought that he had four broken ribs and a fractured left hip plus severe scalp wounds. Twelve years later, x-rays revealed that he had also sustained three fractures of the hipbones plus a hip dislocation. Orville suffered severe pain for the rest of his life from the injuries caused by that accident.

Bishop Wright learned about the accident the following day. He wrote in his diary, "Orville injured. Orville's disaster at 5; Selfridge's death" (Papers 2: 925). A month earlier on August 17, he had written, ". . . Orville started to Washington this evening at 10:12 via Harrisburg, Pa. Both he and Wilbur peril their lives; perhaps Orville most by the unsuitableness of the grounds at Ft. Myer" (Papers 2: 913). It is impossible to know if he had some premonition of the forthcoming disaster, but earlier he had written a letter to Wilbur expressing a similar concern. On August 2, he wrote:

> I think that, aside from the value of your life to yourself and to ourselves, you owe it to the world, that you should avoid unnecessary personal risks. Your death or even becoming a crippled or an invalid, would seriously affect the progress of aeronautical science. [. . .] Soon, others can do the flying, but you have a field for truth and science that no one else can fill. I think that you and Orville ought to take special care of your health, as well as of your lives ("Miracle" 288).

It is obvious that the possibility of serious harm to one of his sons weighed heavily on the bishop's mind. But the Wright family was not given to emotional displays. They were a family given to action and to solving problems.

The day after the crash, even though he was in severe emotional and physical pain, Orville asked Charlie Taylor and Charlie Furman to bring the broken propeller and other pieces from the wreck to the hospital. Already, Orville was trying to figure out what went so wrong.

Octave Chanute had seen the accident and almost immediately said the problem was with the propellers. It was later discovered that a longitudinal crack had developed in the right propeller blade seconds before the crash. It had set in motion a series of events, which ultimately caused Orville to loose control over the functions of the Flyer.

When Orville was asked if he had lost his nerve, he relied, "The only thing I'm afraid of is that I can't get well soon enough to finish the tests this year" (Kelly 232).

Katharine was in Washington by Friday afternoon. Lieutenant Lahm met her at the train station and took her to Fort Myer. Charles Flint, who had come from New York to see Orville fly, took her to see Orville. She was permitted to stay only for twenty minutes.

Octave Chanute helped her draft a letter to the Signal Corps requesting an extension for the completion of the demonstration trials. The Wrights were given until June, 1909, to complete the terms of their contract.

On October 31, Orville and Katharine boarded a train for Dayton. Bishop Wright noted in his diary, "He is brought out from the depot on a wheeled chair. His mind is good as ever and his body promises to be in due time" (Papers 2: 934).

Orville's mind remained clear into his seventies but his body never completely healed. He suffered such severe pain that at times he was bedridden. After a few years, he even stopped flying and seldom took a commercial airliner because the impact of landing set off excruciating pain. But what he achieved at Fort Myer can best be summed up by the words of Major George Squier, the executive officer to the chief of the Signal Corps;

> Of course we deplore the accident, but no one who saw the flights of the last four days at Fort Myers could doubt for an instant that the problem of aerial navigation was solved. If Mr. Wright should never again enter any airplane, his work last week at Fort Myer will have secured him a lasting place in history as the man who showed the world that mechanical flight was an assured success. No one seems to realize at this close range what a revolution the flights portend. The problem is solved, and it only remains to work out the details (Crouch 378).

Octave Chanute had written Wilbur on September 30 that when he had left Orville, "He had recovered his pluck and mental poise; the old genial smile had come back" (Papers 2: 929).

Indeed his pluck had come back. Two months later, while still using a cane, he was on board ship with Katharine, sailing to Europe.

CHAPTER TWENTY-FOUR

TRIALS AND TRIUMPHS

It was a perfect day for flying, "a day of a thousand," Wilbur wrote to Katharine. But because of "poor Selfridge's death," Wilbur didn't feel it "decent to proceed." He had learned about Orville's accident and Lieutenant Selfridge's death just as he was preparing to fly for the Michelin and d'Aviation prizes. He postponed the trials until later in the year.

To the very end of his life, Wilbur remained the older brother. The responsibility of protecting his younger brother was so deeply ingrained in him that, even though he was thousands of miles away with an ocean separating them, Wilbur assumed responsibility for the accident. He was convinced he never should have left Orville to face the American trials alone. He could have protected him from the distracting attentions of the curious. If he had been there, Orville could have paid more attention to preparing the Flyer. He was sure Orville had let the two Charleys attach the new propellers rather than having done the job himself.

The enormous cost of the accident must have weighed heavily on this highly sensitive man. Wilbur had always been guarded in expressing his innermost feelings with anyone except the family. This time was no different. He left the airfield alone and rode out into the countryside. He needed to come to terms with this latest tragedy.

Nine months later he wrote Chanute about the accident. "In so far as the responsibility falls upon anyone I suppose it falls upon me as I did the testing of the [propellers]" (Papers 1: 954).

Yet in some small way this tragedy fanned a flame within Wilbur, which fueled a series of spectacular flights. Four days after Orville's accident, on September 21, he set the world endurance record of one hour, 31 minutes and 25 4/5 seconds. On September 28, he won his first Aero-club de France Aviation Commission prize by flying one hour, seven minutes, and 24 seconds.

The same day he won the Club de France prize, he set a world passenger record by taking Paul Tissandier aloft for an eleven minute, 35 2/3 second ride. He set three more world passenger records: first, by taking Franz Reichel for a 55 minute, 32 2/3 second ride on October 3; then on October 6, he took Arnold Fordyce up for one hour, four minutes and 26 1/5 seconds; and finally, on October 10, he flew for an hour, nine minutes, 45 seconds with Paul Painleve.

Major Baden-Powel, the president of the Aeronautical Society of Great Britain, had seen one of Wilbur's flights in October. He was quoted in the Paris edition of the New York *Herald* as having said:

If only some of our people in England could see or imagine what Mr. Wright is now doing I am certain it would give them a terrible shock. A conquest of the air by any nation means more than the average man is willing to admit or even think about. That Wilbur Wright is in possession of a power that controls the fate of nations is beyond dispute (Kelly 246).

Another member of the British aeronautical society who traveled to France to witness the flights was Griffith Brewer. He found Wilbur surrounded by curious admirers, so he sat down to wait. When one of the helpers came to retrieve a tool, Brewer handed him his card. Wilbur acknowledged the receipt of the card by giving Brewer a nod. Afterwards the two men went to lunch at Madame Pollet's inn. That simple meal and friendly conversation lead to a life-long friendship, which later included Orville.

The first woman to ride in an aeroplane was the wife of Hart Berg, the man who represented the Flint Company in Europe. Mr. Berg was concerned about his wife's long dress blowing in the breeze, so he fastened a rope around her legs. The unusual gait caused by the rope binding her legs became the inspiration for the fashion designer who created the "hobble skirt."

Both royalty and common folk witnessed Wilbur's flights and were enthralled with this latest achievement of man. One of those who had been a passenger and who had enjoined the exhilaration of flight was Major Baden-Powell. He described his experience:

All being ready, coats are buttoned, and caps pulled down to prevent being blown off. [. . .] Then the driver bends down and releases the catch, which holds the anchoring wire. The machine is off. It bounds forward and travels rapidly along the rail. [. . .] When half the rail has been traversed, the lever is pulled back, the planes come into operation, and the whole machine rises almost imperceptibly off the track. The ascent must be very gradual. When the machine leaves the track it glides so close to the ground that one often doubts it is really started in the air, but then it gradually mounts. [. . .]

So steady and regular is the motion that it appears exactly as if it were progressing along an invisible elevated track. Only just now and again, as a swirl of wind catches it, does it make a slight undulation like a boat rising to a big wave. [. . .] All the time the engine is buzzing so loudly and the propellers humming so that after a trip one is almost deaf (Crouch 381).

On November 5, 1908, Wilbur was the guest of honor at a luncheon of the "Autour du Monde," a club comprised of French intellectuals. Later that day he was presented to the French Senate and given a standing ovation. In the evening he was honored at a banquet of over 200 people where he and Orville were awarded gold medals. The medals were the Aero Club of France award and the gold medal of the Academy of Sports. Earlier the brothers had been awarded medals from the International Peace Society.

All of this adulation must have come as quite a surprise to Wilbur because this same Aero Club of France had offered a prize to the flyer who could reach an altitude of 25 meters from an unassisted take-off. That requirement eliminated the Wright Flyer, which was still using the long track and falling weights to achieve lift off.

The Aero Club de Sarthe viewed these rules as a slight to their most honored member, Wilbur Wright; therefore, the club established its own prize of 1,000 francs for an altitude flight of 30 meters.

However, on the night of November 5, all of this turmoil seems to have been forgotten and Wilbur responded to the gracious banquet given in his honor with an insightful acceptance speech. He said:

When we did not know each other, we had no confidence in each other; today, when we are acquainted, it is otherwise: we believe each other, and we are friends. I thank you for this. In the enthusiasm being shown around me, I see not merely an outburst intended to glorify a person, but a tribute to an idea that has always impassioned mankind. I sometimes think that the desire to fly after the fashion of birds is an idea handed down to us by our ancestors who, in their grueling travels across trackless lands in prehistoric times, looked enviously on the birds soaring freely through space, at full speed, above all obstacles, on the infinite highway of the air. [. . .] But it is not really necessary to look too far into the future; we see enough already to be certain that it will be magnificent. Only let us hurry and open the roads (Papers 2: 934).

Almost as if scientists everywhere heard those prophetic words, men have continued to open the roads Wilbur spoke of that night in 1908. Today men are circling the earth in space stations and we are receiving heavenly pictures form the Hubble telescope thanks to the courage of two brothers from a small town in Ohio.

Wilbur was obviously touched by the friendliness extended to him by the French, especially from Leon Bollee and Pellier. But he wrote to Chanute that he longed for some time to himself.

Wilbur continued to outperform himself. On November 13, 1908, he won the Altitude Prize of the Aero-Club of the Sarthe by flying twice as high as required, a height of 70 meters. Then on November 18 he captured the Aero-Club de France prize by flying to the altitude of 25 meters; he met the requirement of an unassisted take-off by lifting off from an extended track.

On November 14, Orville wrote Wilbur from Dayton. Speculating on the cause of his accident. He wrote:

The only explanation I have been able to work out of the cause of the plunge for the ground is that the rear rudder, after the stay wire was torn loose by the propeller, fell over on its side and in some mysterious manner was caught and held in this position, with a pressure on its under side (Papers 2: 937).

Orville's letter clearly demonstrated that he had looked objectively at the accident, considered its causes and moved on with his life. It was a letter filled with hope for the future. Even though Orville's physical recovery progressed slowly, he appeared to have come to terms with his tragic accident.

However, Orville was concerned about Wilbur because on October 5, 1908, Arthur Harmsworth, Lord Northcliffe, the publisher of the London *Daily Mail,* had offered a $5,000 prize to the first person to fly the English Channel. Wilbur was definitely interested. Orville objected to his brother flying the channel without him being available to assist with the preparation of the Flyer. He said it was because Wilbur had had so much trouble with the engine, but it may have been that Orville was concerned about the possibility that Wilbur would be forced down over the channel.

Orville had been to the bicycle shop in his wheelchair and seen that Charlie had finished all the engines and the other work that had needed to be done. He told Wilbur that over five hundred letters remained unanswered, but he was busy designing the forged connecting rod suggested by Wilbur. Unanswered letters would continue to haunt Orville for the rest of his life. Answering letters was a task he hating doing.

The letters between Wilbur and Octave Chanute had continued but they were not nearly as frequent or as filled with technical details as before. Chanute wrote a letter to Paul Renard who had asked what part of the Wright machine came from Chanute and what part came from the brothers. It appears from Chanute's response that he was attempting to be honest, but there appeared to be a point of contention because Chanute claimed that the Wrights, "added the warping of the wings, an idea which I believe was quite personal to them although Mouillard, (before his death) at his (Chanute's) instigation, had patented it . . . in the United States on May 18, 1897. [. . .]" In the same letter he said:

> But the Wrights' most important merits lie in their application of a motor to the glider. They made a study of lifting surfaces in 41 laboratory experiments, the results of which I calculated and which I have preserved. They designed a propeller with a performance superior to ordinary propellers. They thought out a very effective transmission, and designed a sturdy and reliable motor. All this, built with their own hands and put into operation by themselves, at their own risk and peril (Papers 2: 941).

The Wrights had received the U.S. patent on May 22, 1906. It was the basic Wright patent, incorporating the constructions and combinations of the Wright 1902 glider. The question of who had the legal rights to wing warping was heating up.

Once the Wrights began flying in public, the knowledge of wing warping and the other control devices became a public issue. In fact, Wilbur seemed to be showing the French pilots how the plane worked.

As successful as Wilbur was in France, he still missed the companionship of his family. On November 14, he invited Orville, Katharine and "Pop" (the bishop) to come to Europe. He suggested that Orville could supervise and design the machines that would be needed. Orville was still under the care of a masseur, but he would soon exchange his crutches for two canes. He and Katharine planned to leave for Europe the first of January.

While still at Camp d'Auvours, Wilbur had started to train the three pilots required by the French contract. They were Count Charles de Lambert, Paul Tissandier and Captain Lucas de Girardville.

On December 18, Wilbur set a new endurance record of one hour, 54 minutes and 2/5 of a second. That same day he won his third Aero Club de France award by flying to an altitude of 115 meters. His heart was set on winning the Michelin prize, so on December 28 he paid his 50-franc entry fee. On the last day of 1908, snow covered the ground, the temperature was well below freezing and the wind was a bone-chilling cold. Wilbur donned his coat, hat and gloves and climbed into the open air Flyer and ascended into the frigid sky. He remained aloft for 43 minutes but was forced to land because of a broken fuel line.

Wilbur wasn't about to accept defeat. By afternoon the weather had worsened, but still Wilbur was determined. The icy mist surrounded the Flyer as it ascended into the winter sky. He circled the frozen field for two hours, 18 minutes and 33 1/5 seconds until the extreme temperature finally took its toll. He succeeded in claiming the Michelin prize, but it was a tribute to his excellent physical stamina that he didn't develop a severe case of pneumonia in the process.

Wilbur made five more flights before he left for the warmer climate of Pau in southern France. His final passengers were the friends and workmen who had helped him. Wilbur had set nine world records while at Le Mans, the small country village located a hundred miles from Paris.

CHAPTER TWENTY-FIVE

WORLD RECOGNITION

Although the French had warmly received Wilbur, he still yearned for his closest companion in life, his partner in their great adventure of flight, his brother, Orville. As many of their letters indicate, like most brothers, they had their differences, but they seemed to do their best work when they worked together. Carrie Grumbach, their faithful housekeeper, observed that at times they had heated discussions in which each brother argued his own point of view, then was converted to the other brother's way of thinking. The result was that they had exchanged positions. But that was the way they stimulated, challenged and refined their thinking.

Katharine was the third member of the trio. She was a steadying force in their lives. Although she was active in her own profession as a high school teacher, she still managed the household and participated in the women's rights movement. She provided the emotional support they needed when they faced failure and she rejoiced with them when they succeeded. For two men said to be so shy of women, it was their sister that helped them to be at ease in social situations. It is clear from their letters to her that each brother was able to express his own unique sense of humor with her. Even though Katharine was the youngest, and a woman, she was the only one who had graduated from college and was engaged in a profession. But they never appeared to be threatened by this, nor did they seem to feel superior to her because they were men. In fact they each seemed to have taken pride in the accomplishments of the others. There existed an unspoken agreement among the three. They were family: they respected each other, they treated each other as equals (most of the time) and they would always try to be there for each other.

Their reunion at the Paris train depot must have evoked deep emotions among them, but being well-bred mid-westerners, those feelings were most likely expressed only through a warm hug and a hardy handshake. It's not hard to imagine what must have crossed Wilbur's mind when he saw his usually athletic brother walking haltingly with the assistance of a pair of canes. Seeing his always-vibrant younger sister looking subdued and somewhat haggard must have tugged at his tender heart.

Wilbur had his work to do. Part of it would include rehabilitating his two younger siblings. Katharine and Orville would remain in Paris a few days so Katharine could shop and see the sights. Then they would travel to Pau. But even the most carefully laid plans can go awry. On the way to Pau, their train collided with a smaller local train. Two people were killed. They were unharmed except it appeared that Orville had been robbed. Then the missing items were discovered under an overturned mattress.

The people of Pau, a resort town in southern France, had built a large hangar with living quarters and a fully equipped shop for Wilbur and the Flyer. The hangar was so large the Flyer could be moved in and out without removing its front rudder and vertical tail. The mayor had even selected a chef to prepare Wilbur's meals.

Orville and Katharine were provided a suite of rooms at the best hotel in town, Hotel Gassion. Katharine acted as the brothers' social secretary, relieving them of having to remember all their official functions and social engagements. She came well prepared, having brought two modest evening gowns, a rose one and a black one, and a tailored traveling suit. While in Paris she had purchased several fashionable hats and two additional suits. The only jewelry she ever wore was the small diamond ring given her by Orville the day she graduated from Oberlin College

After the Wrights were presented to King Alfonso of Spain, Katharine described him as "a good husband" because he had promised his wife he wouldn't fly even though he was intensely interested in all the functions of the Flyer. He asked many questions about its operation and even sat in the passenger seat, but he kept his promise to his queen and did not fly.

When King Edward of England visited Pau in March, the Wrights were formally presented to him. He was more interested in seeing Wilbur fly than in learning how the Flyer worked. During his visit, Katharine rode for her second time in the Flyer. Before her first flight, Katharine said she had never flown, but she had *heard* a great deal about flying, most likely referring to the many lively discussions her brothers had had.

Wealthy visitors were delighted to be a part of the miracle of flight. Many of them pulled the rope that raised the weights to the peak of the derrick. One of these was the former prime minister of England, Lord Arthur Balfour.

The Europeans were greatly impressed by the Wrights. King Alfonso called Katharine "the perfect American." She had endeared herself to the people by her wit and honesty. Her huge new French chapeaus added to her allure as the mysterious teacher of classical languages. Wilbur was considered appealing to the ladies because of his hawk-like features and athletic gait. While in Le Mans he had even been implicated in a divorce suit, but it was later discovered the offender was one of his mechanics. Orville was still recuperating from his debilitating accident, but even so, at 37, he looked quite debonair with his cane and bowler hat.

Wilbur did not set any new records while in Pau. He was there to train the three French pilots, Paul Tissandier, Paul Lucas-Girardville and Charles de Lambert. Tissandier flew on February 9 and Lucas-Girardville on the nineteenth. De Lambert made a thirty-three minute flight on March 17, but Tissandier surpassed his record by remaining aloft a minute longer that same day.

While in Le Mans, Wilbur had agreed to provide a series of demonstration flights in Rome and to train two Italian pilots. When he finished his work in France, he gave the Flyer to Lazare Weiller and the French syndicate. He had a new Flyer shipped to Pau where it was partially assembled, then shipped to Rome.

On April 1, 1909, Wilbur and Hart Berg went to Rome. Wilbur was impressed with the historic significance of the city. In a letter to Orville, who was in Paris, he wrote that the automobile shop where the Flyer was assembled "is located outside the north gate of the city, on the old Flaminian Way along which Caesar passed on his way to the conquest of Gaul [. . .]" (Papers2: 949).

Kelly comments on events following the assembly of the Flyer:

> It was then moved across the city on a truck drawn by a magnificent team of gray horses to the military field at Centocelle. As the strange-looking machine was carried through the streets past ancient ruins, it is doubtful if amazed beholders had ever seen a greater contrast between old and new (255).

Lieutenant Mario Calderara proved to be an apt student, but his constant cigarette smoking annoyed Wilbur. Calderara would later finish training the second student pilot, Lieutenant Umberto Savoia. On April 24, 1909, the first cameraman ever to record the wonder of flight on a motion picture film rode in the Flyer with Wilbur. His motion picture of the flight gives the viewer the feeling of sitting right next to Wilbur and experiencing flight.

As in Le Mans, notables came to see the breathtaking spectacle of flight: the wealthy American, J. P. Morgan; the Italian King, Victor Emmanuel; Dowager Queen Margherita; and all the Italian cabinet ministers. Captain von Kehler, the managing director of Studien Gesellschaft, an organization for the study of aeronautics, also came. His organization had been conducting experiments on dirigibles. The wealthy men who financed these studies were interested in forming a German Wright company. A preliminary contract was signed. The Wrights would receive cash, stock and a ten per cent royalty on all planes sold.

The Wrights left Rome, the Eternal City, and went to Paris, the City of Lights, and then to Le Mans. There the Aero Club de Sarthe presented the brothers with a magnificent bonze statue designed by Louis Carvin. The statue depicted the Wright brothers standing on the edge of a chasm, gazing upon an eagle in flight with the spirit of aviation hovering above them.

Next, the Wrights traveled to London where they received gold medals from both the Aeronautical Society of Great Britain and from the Aero Club of the United Kingdom. Both honors were given at formal banquets.

They traveled to Battersea to inspect the balloon factory operated by the Short brothers. Charles Stewart Rolls had contracted with the Shorts to construct a Wright Flyer. The Wrights agreed to this arrangement rather than create a new syndicate. The Shorts produced six Wright machines for British customers.

On May 4, 1909, the two Wright brothers and their sister, Katharine, sailed on the German liner, *Kronprinzessin Cecile*. The shrill blaring of ships' whistles and the ringing of boat bells heralded their arrival in New York. Clapping hands and loud cheers accompanied their walk down the gangplank. Finally, America had recognized the Wright brothers as the heroes they were. It had taken the flying demonstrations in Europe to make the country realize the Wrights' extraordinary accomplishment.

A cab carried the Wrights to New York's Waldorf Hotel for a luncheon reception. New York officials had wanted to stage an elaborate homecoming celebration but the governor of Ohio objected because the city officials in Dayton had already planned the Wright Brothers Home Day Celebration for June 17-18.

The Wrights simply wanted to return home and continue to live as quietly as they had before, but they were now celebrities and Dayton wanted to make the most of it. Wilbur complained in a letter to Chanute that this was just an excuse to advertise the city rather than to honor them.

Ten miles from Dayton, Ed Ellis, a friend of Wilbur's, boarded the Wrights' train and presented Katharine with a bouquet of American Beauty long-stem roses. Then he announced that ten thousand people awaited their arrival at the Dayton train station. The falderal was just beginning. Eleven carriages were drawn up at the depot. The Wright brothers were driven home in a carriage drawn by four white horses. Factory whistles blew, a band played and a cannon fired a thirty-gun salute. There were speeches, a reception and a fireworks display.

What the brothers really wanted was to get on with their preparations for the Army trials, which were to have been completed by the end of June. They spent every spare minute either in the bicycle shop or in Lorin's barn working on the Army Flyer. It was to be their fastest plane yet and they had much to do to get it ready on time.

But they also had other business to attend to. At the end of May, they went to the Packard automobile plant in Detroit. There they met with Russell Alger who was interested in starting a company to build the Wright Flyers.

Two weeks later they traveled to Washington to receive the Aero Club of America award from President Taft. In his speech, Taft said that the work of the Wright brothers was something in which all Americans could take pride. In his comments to the brothers, he paraphrased the America expression, "keeping your nose to the grindstone," and said that they had kept their nose at the job and because of this persistence they had been able to solve the problem of flight.

During the luncheon which followed, the brothers told General James Allen of the Signal Corps that the Flyer would be delivered to Ft. Myer by June 28, but they did not see how they could complete the trials by that date. With all the attention being shown the Wrights, it would have been ungracious of General Allen to have forced the issue of the deadline that day. The general gave them an additional month to complete the trials.

June 17 and 18 of 1909 were declared official holidays in Dayton. Schools, factories and public buildings were closed to honor Dayton's hometown heroes. At 9:00 a.m. on June 17, every factory whistle in town blew and every church bell rang and the cannon on the riverbank boomed. The brothers left their shop and listened to the noisy racket for ten minutes until calm returned again to the city. But it didn't remain calm for long. At 10:00, a carriage appeared at the bicycle shop. In it were Ed Sines, Orville's old partner in the printing business, and Ed Ellis, friend of Wilbur and now assistant city auditor. The two men accompanied the brothers to Van Cleve Park for a pageant. When it was time for the brothers to speak, Wilbur performed the task for both of them. He rose and said, "Thank you, gentlemen" and sat down again.

Back at the shop, Wilbur and Orville covered the windows with canvas hoping to get at least some work done. In the afternoon, the fire department had a parade and drill during which the brothers were given the keys to the city. Once that was over, they hurried back to the shop for more work. At 8:00 they were given a reception at the YMCA followed by a fireworks display "featuring the blazing portraits of Wilbur and Orville entwined in a smoking American flag" (Howard 297). That was Thursday.

On Friday all fifteen of the Wright family (spouses and children of Lorin and Reuchlin included) were seated on the homecoming speakers' platform. Bishop Wright gave the invocation. One thousand school children wearing red, white and blue sat on bleachers behind the family. The children formed the American flag and sang patriotic songs.

General Allen had come from Washington and presented both brothers with the Congressional Medal of Honor. Governor Cox presented them with gold medals from the Ohio Legislature and Mayor Burkhardt gave them diamond-studded medals from the city of Dayton. Then in the afternoon there was a parade consisting of transportation floats and another spectacular automobile parade in the evening featuring a car strung with electric lights driven by a family friend.

A gift of a player piano was delivered to the house on Hawthorne Street and was apparently enjoyed by the family even though they all knew it was just an advertising gimmick.

CHAPTER TWENTY-SIX

A SECOND TIME AT FORT MYER

After the completion of the time consuming celebrations in Dayton, the brothers were on the train to Washington, D.C.. Charlie Taylor was already there uncrating the parts of the new Wright Flyer. Besides Charlie there were two army officers to help them, Lieutenant Frank Lahm and Lieutenant Benjamin Foulois. Orville had designed a new control stick called the split-handle lever. The Flyer was assembled by June 28.

Congress had been invited by the Signal Corps to witness the maiden flight of the new Flyer, but a 16 mile per hour wind kept the flying machine grounded for the day and Congress was disappointed. Many of the papers claimed that the Wrights snubbed Congress by not flying, even though their cancelled flight was due to the strong the wind that day. The first flight of the Flyer the following day was also a great disappointment. One flight after another ended poorly, but the worst was yet to come. On July 2, while Orville was airborne for only eight minutes, the motor stalled. Then, when Orville was gliding in for a landing, the machine collided with a dead thorn tree. The sharp thorns ripped through the wing covering and broke several ribs. The Flyer hit the ground so hard it broke the skids. The spectators went crazy. They rushed onto the field and stripped the thorn tree bare. Orville was badly shaken, but he walked away from the accident unaided. When Wilbur spotted a man taking pictures of the downed machine, he raced over and demanded the photographic plates. Later he returned them with an apology, because the man was from the War Department and was documenting the accident.

While Charlie and Wilbur repaired the broken ribs and skids, Orville returned to Dayton to make the new wing covering. When flight was resumed on July 9, the bad luck seemed to continue; the motor ran poorly, two skids were broken and repaired, then a violent windstorm arose and blew down the large tent which had been erected for the president and his cabinet.

Finally on Saturday morning the spell was broken. Orville started to fly about 7 p.m. and remained airborne for seventeen minutes. He soared over the parade ground, over the cavalry stables and over the huge smokestack of the Fort Myer's powerhouse. Then on Monday, July 19, he circled the field twenty-five times in his first flight and twenty-eight, in his second flight. After that, there was no stopping him. On Tuesday he broke the U.S. endurance record and flew for one hour, 20 minutes and 45 seconds. During his flight he reached an altitude of 300 feet and flew three figure eights to the amazement of all. The next day he demonstrated the versatility of the new Army machine by circling the parade ground twenty-one times and by flying circles of only 200 feet in diameter.

Washington was smitten. The population swarmed across the Potomac River. Young and old, wealthy and poor, high brow and low brow, they all wanted to see this wonder, the Wright Flyer streaming across the heavens with the famous Orville wielding the controls. Orville obliged President Taft and Vice-President James Sherman by flying in a 15 mile-an-hour wind.

But there were trials to complete: an endurance trial with a passenger and a speed trial also with a passenger. Tuesday, July 27, was not very promising. Heavy black clouds covered the sky, 25 mile per hour winds battered the crowd, then the heavens opened and drenched the 10,000 spectators waiting for the flight. Finally, the wind and rain stopped, the shed door opened and the Flyer was moved to its track. At 6:30 p.m., Orville and his passenger, Lieutenant Lahm, climbed into the Flyer. At 6:35 President Taft arrived and stood with the members of his cabinet. A minute later, Orville was airborne with his passenger. He circled and circled and circled until he had circled the field seventy-nine times. He set a new world endurance record for carrying a passenger. Wilbur had set the record at 1 hour, 9 minutes and 41 seconds at Camp d'Auvours on October 10, 1908. Orville beat that. His record was 1 hour, 12 minutes and 37 4/5 seconds. Wilbur was so happy that Orville had his confidence back that he did a little dance right in the center of the field. The crowd went wild.

The next day was July 28, the day the contract was scheduled to expire. There was one more requirement to fulfill, the speed test. Orville had already decided that the best course would be a flight to Alexandria, Virginia, and back. Lieutenant Foulois was chosen as the navigator and official observer. The Wrights were given three additional days to finish. That day, the wind was so strong the marker balloons were blown away. The next day a violet squall came up.

WILBUR WRIGHT TIMING THE FLIGHT AT FORT MYER

On Friday, July 30, the weather was little better. Orville waited. Finally the weather cleared. The president arrived. The Flyer was put on the launching track. Both Orville and Wilbur fussed with this and that for over half an hour. Then Lieutenant Foulois, armed with two stopwatches, a box compass, an aneroid barometer and a map of Northern Virginia, climbed into the passenger seat. Orville climbed in beside him. The weights were lowered, the Flyer started down the track, slowly at first, then it picked up speed, skimming over the grasses of the parade ground. It gradually gained altitude and soared into the sky. It circled the field twice then headed to the starting line. Wilbur threw the signal flag to the ground with one hand and started his stopwatch with the other hand. At the same time members of the Aeronautical Board started their stopwatches. In the air, Lieutenant Foulois had clicked on his stopwatch. The official time would be the average of all the times registered on all those stopwatches.

Orville had to be mindful of the gusting winds. The wind had blown the turning marker too low for Orville to spot and he flew right past it. The crowd on Shuter's Hill went wild when Orville flew back into sight. As he rounded the balloon, Foulois clicked on his second stopwatch. Orville raised the Flyer to 400 feet, setting a new altitude record, but then a downdraft pushed the Flyer lower. Orville worked the controls until they had again regained altitude.

When the Flyer failed to appear at the finish line at the time Wilbur had estimated, he got concerned. He was relieved when it finally came into view. Then suddenly it disappeared. Within minutes it reappeared, to the great relief of the 7,000 spectators who were waiting on the parade grounds. Orville picked up speed and passed over the finish line. All the stopwatches clicked for the last time. Everyone held their breath until the dust cleared and they could see that Orville and his passenger were safe. Then the crowd rushed towards the Flyer. Wilbur was ecstatic. Orville was jubilant. He was back flying and loving it.

The official average speed was calculated at 42.58 miles-per-hour. On August 2, 1909, the U. S. War Department accepted the Wright Flyer. The Wrights received $30,000, $25,000 the agreed upon price and a bonus of $2,500 for each of the two full miles over the forty miles-per-hour required in the contract. It had been a costly proposition for both the U.S. Government and the Wright brothers.

CHAPTER TWENTY-SEVEN

STRIKING BACK

Despite the Wrights' monumental achievements, it had taken the world over five years to comprehend what they had done. Those should have been one of the most exhilarating times in their lives, but they weren't. Just as they received world acclaim, others emerged who used the Wrights' technology and started to take from them both the glory and financial gain due them.

This did not sit well with them. For years they had devoted all their available resources and risked their very lives to solve the problems of flight. Early in the process, they had been very generous in sharing their discoveries. But as they came closer to a solution, they were more guarded with their information and shared the results of their experiments with only two trusted friends, Chanute and George Spratt. By that time they had realized that knowing how to build a plane that could actually fly could become a source of income for them. A month after their Kitty Hawk success, they had begun the patent process. But it had taken until May 1906 to be granted their patent. Once they had developed a practical flying machine, they tried to market it, but they had no success for the first two years and, then, only limited success. Others were flying and many were using the Wrights' lateral control system without obtaining the license for its use. Since the control system had been patented in the United States and in Europe, using an aeroplane with that lateral control system for exhibition and commercial purposes required a license. However, if the system were used for experimental purposes, no license was required.

Had Chanute been right all along? He had urged them to fly in exhibitions such as the St. Louis Fair. Should they have flown for trophies and prizes as Glenn Curtiss, who won the *Scientific American* trophy, had done? They could have won most of those contests, yet they had chosen to pursue government contracts instead. Once those were secured, they needed to spend their time filling contracts, not exhibition flying.

This was a time of intense emotional activity; it must have resembled an emotional roller coaster. They were exhilarated by the success they had attained. Yet, at the same time, they were angry because others were claiming what they had worked so hard to achieve. Although Orville had set records at Fort Myers, others were also flying and having their own successes. The French aviator, Henri Bleroit, became the first man to fly the English Channel on July 26, 1909. Glenn Curtiss won his second *Scientific American* trophy on July 17 by flying for 56 minutes.

The Wrights had known Curtiss since 1906 when he was a guest in their home. Curtiss manufactured motorcycle motors and Tom Baldwin, a balloonist, used one of the Curtiss motors to propel the balloon he was flying at a fair in Dayton. Curtiss had come to Dayton to make repairs on the motor. While there, the two men met the Wrights and were invited to their home. All the men were interested in aviation and spent the whole evening deep in discussion about "propellers, airships, flying machines and motors."

When Curtiss had joined the Aerial Experiment Association (AEA) at the invitation of Alexander Graham Bell, he wrote the Wrights telling them that he was studying aeronautics and offered to give them a motor. They were building their own and declined his offer. As the director of experiments, Curtiss was responsible for the construction of *June Bug,* the AEA plane, which he flew for his first *Scientific American* trophy. Lieutenant Selfridge, secretary of the AEA, had written the Wrights for information, that was used in constructing the machine. The Wrights had responded to Selfridge's letter by citing Wilbur's two published speeches given before the Western Engineers Association and the information contained in their patent, which was on file at the U.S. Patent Office in Washington, D.C.

After Curtiss had won the *Scientific American* trophy by flying the AEA's *June Bug,* Orville wrote to Curtiss. In his letter of July 20, 1908, he wrote:

> Claim 14 of our patent . . . specifically covers the combination which we are informed you are using (movable surfaces at the tips of the wings, adjustable to different angles on the right and left sides for maintaining lateral balance). [. . .] If it is your desire to enter exhibition business, we would be glad to take up the matter of a license to operate under our patent for that purpose" (Papers 2: 907).

Curtiss became disillusioned with the constraints of the AEA and set up a company with Augustus Herring, Chanute's associate who had tested his gliders at the Wrights' camp in Kitty Hawk in 1902. Herring claimed that he owned patents which would circumvent the Wrights' patents. Curtiss accepted Herring's word and offered his expert knowledge of motors and his factory in Hammondsport, New York, as his contribution to the business deal. Herring enticed the president of the Aero Club of America, Cortlandt Bishop, to invest in the new company. Glenn Curtiss invited his friend, Judge Monroe Wheeler, to join the company. Wheeler was elected president of the board of directors for the new company and Cordtlandt Bishop and Tom Baldwin also became members of the board. In February 1909, the Herring-Curtiss Company was chartered in the state of New York.

Their first customer was the Aero Club of New York, which commissioned them to build a flying machine for $5,000. This plane violated the Wrights' patent just as the *June Bug* had done. Curtiss flew the new machine, *The Golden Flier,* on June 26 at the Morris racetrack before a paying audience. When he flew it again on July 17, he won his second *Scientific American* trophy.

In early August, 1909, just shortly after the Fort Myer's flights, Orville and Katharine went to New York. While there, Orville read an article in New York's *Herald,* which seems to have been the last straw. Glenn Curtiss had been chosen by the Aero Club of America to represent the United States at the International Air Races to be held in Reims, France, in August.

In a letter to Wilbur written on their steam liner, the *Kronprinzessin Cecilie,* on August 10, 1909, Orville wrote:

I think best plan is to start suit against Curtiss, Aeronautic Society, etc., at once. This will call attention of public to fact that the machine is an infringement of ours. Mr. Cordley (Flint Company) favors starting suits in Europe at once and prosecuting them vigorously (Papers 2: 961).

Wilbur returned to Washington to discuss with their attorney, Mr. Toulmin, the possibility of bringing lawsuits against the infringers. He traveled to New York and filed suit against the Aeronautics Society and then went to Hammondsport where he filed a second suit against Curtiss and the Herring-Curtiss Company. This was the beginning of a series of the lawsuits which would cost the Wrights dearly.

Orville wrote Wilbur from Berlin suggesting that an announcement be made stating that anyone connected with a flying machine which violated their patent rights would be sued.

At the time, Orville was flying at Templehofer field, just outside Berlin. His flights so thrilled the German people that they rushed onto the field after each flight just to touch their new hero.

ORVILLE WRIGHT TAKING OFF IN FLYER

The German Emperor, Kaiser Wilhelm, invited Katharine and Orville to be present at the maiden flight of Count von Zeppelin's new dirigible. As the silver airship floated into view, every church bell in Berlin rang and a crowd of 100,000 spectators jammed into the parade ground to greet it.

When Orville was presented to the Count, he invited Orville to accompany him in the dirigible for a flight from Frankfurt to Mannheim. Orville accepted, but, after landing in Mannheim, he was separated from his interpreter, Captain Alfred Hildebrandt. The captain had arranged the Wrights' German flights for the Berlin newspaper, *Lokal-Anzeiger*. Orville was scheduled to appear at an honorary luncheon, but had forgotten the name of the hotel and, not knowing much German, was unable to ask for help. Luckily, a member of the welcoming committee recognized him from his pictures and drove him to the hotel.

Orville finished his flights at Templehofer field in mid September, 1909. He had flown magnificently, setting new records and thrilling all the Germans who had seen his flights. He set a one-man endurance record of one hour and 46 minutes. Then he raised the altitude record from 100 meters to 172 meters. He broke his own record by flying with a passenger for one hour and 35 minutes.

While he was in Berlin, the young Crown Prince Friedrick Wilhelm, then in his twenties, called Orville on the telephone and asked him when he was coming to Potsdam to train pilots. The prince wasn't interested in the pilot training; what he wanted was a ride in the flying machine. Orville had been cautioned that he shouldn't take the prince for a flight without the Kaiser's permission.

At Potsdam, Orville flew before the royal family and their guests. Each time he met a member of the royal family, Orville said he would soon be giving the prince a ride. When no one objected, he decided it was safe to grant the prince's request. On October 2, the prince put on his overcoat and climbed into the Flyer beside Orville. The flight lasted fifteen minutes. Orville flew to an altitude of 100 meters, but the prince wanted him to go higher. Not wanting to anger the Kaiser, Orville decided in favor of caution.

The young prince was so thrilled with his flying experience that he gave Orville his own stickpin which was set in diamonds and rubies. The prince told Orville the "W" on the stickpin could stand for Wright. He was the first royal person ever to fly. Kaiser Wilhelm realized the importance of the aeroplane. He was well aware that it would very likely revolutionize warfare.

While Orville was flying in Germany, Glenn Curtiss was making his mark at the air meet in Reims. The only other non-French pilot to compete was George Cockburn from England. Henri Farman won the 50,000-franc Grand Prix by setting a world endurance record of 3 hours and five minutes. Curtiss had constructed a plane with a 50 horsepower V8 motor just to compete at this race. His closest competitor in the race for the coveted Gorden Bennett trophy was Henri Bleroit; Curtiss won the race by 5.6 seconds.

Curtiss continued to fly for a time in Europe, winning additional prizes and honors before he returned to America in time to fly in the Hudson-Fulton Celebration in New York.

By the time Curtiss left for Europe, his association with Herring had become strained, Herring had not live up to the agreement he made when the company was formed. He was to turn over to the company his patents and other items from his business, in exchange for the voting majority in the company stock. His only contribution had been to suggest some construction changes, which proved to be useless, and to annoy the factory workers by criticizing their work.

Curtiss, Bishop and Wheeler had never checked on Herring's alleged patents. Finally, in October, Herring was ordered by the company board to produce his patents and the other items from his former business.

Herring had never obtained any American patents of his own. It had all been another one of his elaborate schemes. By the time the company declared bankruptcy in December 1910, Herring had already conned W. Starling Burgess, a builder of yachts, into signing a contract with him. When the two planes constructed by this company were wrecked, Burgress bought out Herring's contract. Curtiss, now free of his devious partner, set up a new company, Curtiss Motor Company. Unfortunately the lawyers who handled Glenn Curtiss' legal matters failed to dissolve the Herring-Curtiss Company and Herring still held 2,000 shares of stock. In 1918, Herring sued Curtiss and his associates for five million dollars. The case was settled in favor of Curtiss, but Herring appealed. The final suit was settled out of court after both men had died.

The day after Curtiss returned from the Reims' races on September 21, 1909, he was to begin flying in the Hudson-Fulton Celebration, as was Wilbur Wright. Herring had accepted $5,000 to put the *Reims Racer* on display at the Wannamaker's Department Store in New York immediately upon its return to the United States. That forced Curtiss to fly in an untried plane with a 24 horsepower motor.

When Curtiss arrived on Governors Island where both men had hangers, he stopped at Wilbur's hangar and the two talked about the Reims races. Grover Loening who later became an aeronautical engineer, was present at this meeting. He noticed that Wilbur declined to shake Curtiss' hand because he said they were full of grease. Yet when Guglielmo Marconi, the inventor of the wireless, insisted on shaking Wilbur's hand, grease and all, Wilbur obliged.

On Wednesday, September 29, Curtiss made a brief flight at 7 a.m. which was seen only by two witnesses. Wilbur had strapped a red canoe between the skids of the Flyer to act as a floatation device in case the Flyer had to put down in the water. He tested the Flyer to see if there was any difficulty in handling the addition. When he found no problem, he announced he would fly that day.

It had been previously arranged that the Marconi wireless would transmit a signal to the warships with receiving sets and they, in turn, would use signal flags to alert the other ships that a flight was to begin. Flags were flown on Governors Island to alert other observers who flew flags to alert the residents of Manhattan. Soon the banks of the Hudson River were overflowing with thousands of spectators hoping to catch a glimpse of the white and silver Flyer as it soared above the river. Wilbur had said he would just make a short trip over the ships in the harbor. But once in the air, Wilbur turned his Flyer left and headed toward the Statue of Liberty. As the Flyer soared higher and higher, the ships' passengers realized where Wilbur was headed. The exuberance of the moment was expressed by the resounding ships' bells and the earsplitting foghorn blasts that filled the air. As Wilbur circled the Statue of Liberty, the *Lusitania* was steaming past. Hundreds of its passengers waved handkerchiefs and hats as Wilbur flew overhead.

High winds kept both Curtiss and Wilbur from flying for the next four days. Curtiss was unable to fulfill his commitment to fly from Governors Island to Grant's Tomb. On Monday he shipped his aeroplane to St. Louis where Herring had arranged for him to fly, beginning October 6.

Wilbur announced he would make the twenty-five mile flight Curtiss had been unable to make. The signal was sent across the wireless; the flags were raised. Thousands of New York citizens flocked to the riverside. Two American flags were attached to the Flyer's front rudder; a life jacket was strapped to the lower wing. The silver and white Flyer ascended into the sky accompanied by cheers from the 300 soldiers stationed on Governors Island.

WILBUR WRIGHT TAKING OFF FROM GOVERNOR'S ISLAND

As the Flyer soared over the river, sailors swarmed onto the decks of their ships. Whistles blew, foghorns blared and bells clanged when the Flyer flew over the vessels on the river. Flying was challenging, even dangerous, because of the rising gases from all the ships. Wilbur made a 180-degree turn north of Grant's Tomb and headed back down the river. It took him 33 minutes and 33 seconds to make the twenty-five mile flight, which was seen by a million people. A broken cylinder head prevented any more flights. That was his last public flight.

Wilbur went from New York to Washington where he trained the army pilots, Lieutenant Lahm and Lieutenant Humphrey. Lieutenant Foulois was in France, but he returned in time to have three lessons from Wilbur before he left Washington.

While Wilbur was in New York, he received a visit from Clinton R. Peterkin. At fifteen, Peterkin had worked for J. P. Morgan as an office boy. Now at twenty-four, he was ready to make a name for himself. He proposed starting an American Wright Company. Wilbur told him he was only interested if Peterkin could get "men of affairs" interested in the idea.

It wasn't long until Peterkin had assembled an impressive list of investors: J. P. Morgan, Elbert Gary, Cornelius Vanderbilt, Augustus Belmont, Morton Plant, Thomas Ryan and Theodore P. Shorts. Wilbur returned to New York. He requested that Russell and Fred Algar of the Packard Car Company and Robert Collier be approached. Morgan and Gary withdrew because of objections from the other investors.

The proposal Peterkin made to the Wright brothers was very generous for the times. They would receive $100,000 for their patent rights and expertise, one third of the total shares and a ten per cent royalty on all machines sold. The Wrights accepted his proposal. The new company owned the patent rights and was responsible for prosecuting the infringers of the patent. This relieved the Wrights of all legal expenses.

On November 22, 1909, the Wright Company was incorporated under the laws of New York. Wilbur was president; Orville and Andrew Freedman were the vice-presidents. The members of the board of directors were August Belmont, Robert J. Collier, Cornelius Vanderbilt and Russell Alger.

Both brothers hoped that now they could return to experimenting. Neither of them could have anticipated the length of the infringements suits or how emotionally and physically draining they would be.

CHAPTER TWENTY-EIGHT

TAKING SIDES

With the initiation of the patent suits, two distinct factions emerged. The purists thought it inappropriate for the Wrights to claim any financial compensation for the time, energy, ingenuity, risk and expense that the invention of the first successful heavier-than-air flying machine had cost them. But there were those who thought it reasonable and honorable that the Wrights should profit financially from their invention. The Wrights were forced to provide both substantial evidence in court and to defend their actions to friends and foes alike.

Perhaps one of the most painful interchanges was the one between the Wrights and Octave Chanute. Over a ten-year period, Wilbur and Chanute had exchanged over five hundred letters beginning with Wilbur's first letter of May 13, 1900.

By the time Wilbur wrote that first letter, he and Orville had read all the works recommended by the assistant secretary of the Smithsonian, Richard Rathbun. These included works by Octave Chanute, Samuel Langley and *The Aeronautical Annuals* for 1895, 1896, and 1897 edited by James Means. They also had read four Smithsonian pamphlets, each written by a different pioneer of flight: Louis-Pierre Mouillard, Otto Lilienthal, Samuel Langley and E.C. Huffaker. Before writing to the Smithsonian, they had already read everything they found concerning the flight of birds and in the early field of aeronautics.

Not only had they read all of these works, but also they had begun to evolve their own theory on how to maintain equilibrium in flight. They knew from observing birds that those aerial acrobats adjusted their wings in flight. They had thought about constructing wings which could rotate on a shaft. The wings would have to be constructed in three sections with the center section remaining rigid. They rejected this idea because the craft would be too heavy to fly.

Wilbur accidentally discovered the next idea when he was absentmindedly twisting an inner tube box. That was wing warping. Years later, Orville told William E. Shea, who was working with Mark Sullivan on *Our Times:*

It was not the revelation of a basic principle- it was merely a better mechanical embodiment of a basic principle, which we had already discussed for several months. The basic idea was the adjustment of the wings on the right and left sides to different angles so as to secure different lifts on the opposite sides (Papers 1: 9).

The model they built was successfully tested as a kite in July, 1899. The brothers then decided to build a "man-carrying machine embodying the principle of lateral control used in the kite model already flown" (Papers 1: 12).

In both November and December of 1899, Wilbur had written the U.S. Weather Bureau asking for information on wind velocities for Chicago and vicinities for the months of August, September and November.

Six months later, Wilbur wrote his first letter to Octave Chanute. By this time the Wrights had already developed and tested their wing warping mechanism. In this letter Wilbur wrote Chanute that he was using a "double-deck" machine similar to the one Chanute used in his 1896-1897 experiments, but with the cross-stays removed so that "the whole upper plane may be moved forward or backward, to attain longitudinal equilibrium." He further stated:

> Lateral equilibrium is gained by moving one end more than the other or by moving them in opposite directions. If you will make a square cardboard tube two inches in diameter and eight to ten inches long and choose two sides for your planes you will at once see the torsional effect of moving one end of the plane forward and the other backward, and how this effect is attained without sacrificing lateral stiffness (Papers 1: 18).

In this first letter Wilbur asked Chanute for two things. He asked him to suggest a suitable place to experiment and where could he find information on Pilcher's experiments. (Pilcher was an English engineer who was killed experimenting with one of his gliders.)

It wasn't until December 6, 1902, that Chanute sent the Mouillard patents to the Wrights. Wilbur acknowledged their receipt in his December 11, 1902 letter to Chanute and in the very next sentence said, "We have our patent specifications about complete and hope to have them filed soon" (Papers 1: 290).

By that time the Wrights had built and tested gliders in 1900, 1901 and 1902. They were thinking about building a machine "much larger and about twice as heavy as our present machine. [. . .] And if we find it under satisfactory control in flight, we will proceed to mount a motor" (Papers 1: 290).

Chanute had already talked to Samuel Langley about the Wrights' control mechanism. In a letter to Chanute, Langley wrote on December 7, 1902: "I should be very glad to hear more of what the Wright brothers have done, and especially their means of control, which you think better than the Penard" (Papers 1: 290).

There were questions that still remain unanswered. Why, if Chanute thought that wing warping had already been developed and patented by Mouillard, didn't he say so right from the beginning? Why was it only years later in a letter to Paul Renard, technical editor of *Le Mois*, on November 22, 1908, did he make this statement?

> They added the warping of the wings, an idea which I believe was quite personal to them, although Mouillard, at my instigation had patented it [. . .] in the United States on May 18, 1897 - the doubtful result of his experiment of 1896, and his late death in 1897 [. . .] (Papers 2: 971).

He seemed conflicted about the origin of wing warping. He alluded to this patent in a letter to Ernest L. Jones, publisher of *Aeronautics*:

> I think the Wrights have made a blunder by bringing suit at this time. Not only will this antagonize very many persons but also it may disclose some

prior patents, which will invalidate their more important claims (Papers 2: 962).

Chanute wrote in another letter to Jones in 1900, after Wilbur had first written him, he had given the Wrights "full details and a copy of Mouillard's patent." Yet it wasn't until December 1902, that he sent the patent.

According to Orville's diary entry on January 22, 1904, Chanute had come to see them the same day they had given their patent case to the attorney, Harry A. Toulmin. It seems very likely that they would have talked to Chanute about that when he came to Dayton.

But in the September 21, 1909, letter to Jones, Chanute spoke about Mouillard's patent and stated, "His patent clearly covers the warping of the wings."

Chanute wrote in a letter to Glenn Curtiss' attorney that the concept of warping the wings was very old. He also mentions several experimenters who had taken out patents in France. The most important parts of this letter were the statements, "The bare idea of warping and twisting the wings is old, but there are several ways of accomplishing it" and "It will be for the experts to determine what are equivalent devices" (Papers 2: 967). Once again we note Chanute's conflicting statements.

Even though, from the very first letter, Wilbur had told Chanute about their device for wing warping, Chanute never seemed to understand that what Mouillard had proposed was to turn down one corner by hand in order to turn. What the Wrights developed was a means of controlling the balance of the machine, something entirely different from what Mouillard had suggested. There seemed to be more to Chanute's motives than just misunderstanding, which would come out later.

ORVILLE WRIGHT DEMONSTRATING WING WARPING

Wilbur was aware that fame brings many friends, some true and some just wanting the glory of associating with a famous person. Two of the friends that he and Orville had confided in over the many years of their struggles had been Octave Chanute and George Spratt. Both seemed to turn on them. Wilbur attributes Chanute's antagonism to his advancing age, but George Spratt's disenchantment must have come as a complete surprise. It seems to have been Spratt's opinion that the Wrights had not given him credit for the suggestion that lift and drift should be measured in relationship to each other rather than measuring them separately.

Wilbur was both shocked and hurt. He considered this suggestion a swap of ideas among friends. The Wrights did measure lift and drift in relationship to each other during their wind tunnel experiments. But they had developed Spratt's suggestion into a theory and tested that theory. They had done all the work themselves such as constructing the wind tunnel, making the balances and measuring devices, and conducting experiments on 200 miniature airfoils (wings). The question was, who deserves the credit, the one who thinks of the idea or the one who develops and proves the theory?

Wilbur felt that they had repaid their debt by furnishing Spratt with the results of all these experiments. But Wilbur so valued Spratt's friendship that he offered to give him any scientific information or practical experience they had.

Wilbur even asked Spratt to come to College Park, where he was training the army pilots, so they could talk and hopefully resolve their misunderstanding. Wilbur wanted to maintain the friendship which had provided many pleasant hours at Kitty Hawk. He ended this letter with, "Believe me ever your friend."

The conflict never was resolved. Years after Wilbur's death, when Orville was trying to write an account of their work, he asked Spratt for Wilbur's letters. Once again Spratt brought up all his grievances. Orville never pursued the matter any further.

Relationships between the Wrights and Octave Chanute were still friendly enough in early December1909, for Wilbur to write a detailed letter to Chanute in which he discussed the current infringement suit against Glenn Curtiss and the Herring-Curtiss Company. He wrote:

> The affidavit filed by Mr. Herring is thoroughly characteristic of him. He has suddenly discovered that he invented in 1894 the method of controlling lateral balance by setting surfaces to different angles of incidence on the right and left sides of the machine and correcting the difference in their resistances by means of an adjustable tail (Kelly 354).

The opposition to the Wrights was heating up. On December 12, 1909, the New York *World* published an article in which the aeronautical editor, Arnold Kruckman, wrote: "Their (the Wrights) persistent failure to acknowledge their monumental indebtedness to the man (Chanute) who gave them priceless assistance has been one of the most puzzling mysteries in their career" (Kelly 354).

Wilbur wrote to Kruckman on December 21, saying they had used the Chanute double-decker as the model for obtaining the strongest and lightest flying surface. He refuted the notion that wing warping was an idea suggested by Chanute. Then he wrote:

> Mr. Chanute's sympathetic interest in our work was one of the chief stimulants, which kept us at work till we attained success. We therefore

owe him a great debt of gratitude which we have not the least thought or wish to repudiate. Without it we might have quit and failed. [. . .] For many years we entrusted to him many of our most important secrets, and only discontinued it when we began to notice that his advancing years made it difficult for him to exercise the necessary discretion (Papers 2: 972).

Nearly a month later Wilbur wrote Chanute another letter concerning the article in the New York *World*. He wrote:

The New York *World* has published several articles in the past few months in which you are represented as saying that our claim [. . .] cannot be maintained, as this idea was well known in the art when we began our experiments. As this opinion is quite different from what you expressed in 1901 when we became acquainted with you, I do not know whether it is mere newspaper talk or whether it really represents your present views (Papers 2: 979).

Chanute replied, "I did tell you in 1901 that the mechanism by which your surfaces were warped was original with yourselves" (Papers 2: 981). He said he had given the Wrights the Mouillard patent in 1901 and that in his opinion their claim was limited to the method they used to achieve wing warping, not the idea itself.

Then he brought up a statement made by Wilbur at a dinner speech in which Wilbur, in referring to Chanute, had used the phase "turned up" at their shop. Chanute objected to this casual statement and felt that what Wilbur reported was that he had pushed himself upon them, which was not true.

Wilbur had been nursing some sore spots of his own. Chanute's attack opened up those old wounds. He fired back enumerating all his grievances. Some are worth noting because they explain many of the Wrights' actions and their difficulty in following Chanute's suggestion that they fly for prize money.

It appears that the Wrights were in conflict about sharing the information in their patent and felt they were forced to exploit the patent information and require a license for it's use because they had so little commercial success with selling their plane. Wilbur wrote:

We believed that the physical and financial risks which we took, and the value of the service to the world, justified sufficient compensation to enable us to live modestly with enough surplus income to permit the devotion of our future time to scientific experimenting instead of business. We spent several years of valuable time trying to work out plans, which would have made us independent without hampering the invention by commercial exploitation of the patents. It was only when we found that the sale of the patents offered the only way to obtain compensation for our labors of 1900-1906 that we finally permitted the chance of making the invention free to the world to pass from our hands. [. . .] We honestly think that our work of 1900-1906 has been and will be of value to the world, and that the world owes us something as inventors, regardless of whether we personally make Roman holidays for accident-loving crowds (Papers 2: 983).

This certainly answers the question, why didn't the Wrights capitalize immediately on their invention by flying at exhibitions before people who simply wanted to see the latest daredevil exhibition. The Wrights were serious experimenters, not entertainers, and they had no wish to be perceived as such.

Toward the end of the letter Wilbur wrote:

I expect that we will always continue to disagree in many of our opinions just as we have done ever since our first acquaintance began [. . .] but such differences need not disturb a friendship which has existed so long. [. . .] If anything can be done to straighten matters out to the satisfaction of both you and us, we are not only willing, but anxious (Papers 2: 984).

It is interesting to note that, in 1903, just weeks after the first flight, Chanute read a paper to the American Association for the Advancement of Science, which was later published in *Popular Science Monthly*. In his speech he said, "Being accomplished mechanics, they designed and built the apparatus, applying thereto a new and effective mode of control of their own (Kelly 363). It seems that at the time Chanute thought the system which the Wrights developed was unique to them. It is a mystery why he changed his mind.

Another person who had been supportive of the Wrights was Dr. Alfred Zahm who taught mathematics and physics at Catholic University in Washington, D.C. Dr. Zahm wrote the Wrights offering his services as a technical advisor in the Wright versus Curtiss infringement suit. When the Wrights did not employ him, he became an advisor to Glenn Curtiss and eventually turned against the Wrights. Wilbur was still hoping that they could remain friends when he wrote him:

We do not think that such service carried out in a spirit of fairness need interrupt the friendship which has always existed between us. [. . .] We take the matter as philosophically as possible even when we find good friends lined up against us ("Miracle" 369).

When Wilbur had not heard from Chanute by April he wrote him.

I realize that few friendships are able to stand the strain of frankness, but I believe that it would be better to discuss matters freely than to permit small misunderstandings to gradually grow into big ones by neglect. My object was not to give offense, but to remove it. [. . .] It is our wish that anything, which might cause bitterness should be eradicated as soon as possible (Papers 2: 991).

Two weeks later Chanute wrote that he had been in bad health, and then he wrote:

I have never given out the impression, either in writing or speech, that you had taken up aeronautics at my insistence or were, as you put it, pupils of mine. I have always written and spoken of you as original investigators and worthy of the highest praise. [. . .] The difference in opinion between us, i.e. whether the warping of the wings was in the nature of a discovery by yourselves or had already been proposed and experimented by others, will have to be passed upon by others, but I have always said that you are entitled to immense credit for devising apparatus by which it has been reduced to successful practice. I hope, upon my return from Europe, that we will be able to resume our former relations (Papers 2: 995).

This was the last letter Wilbur ever received from Chanute, who had traveled to Europe for his health. Unfortunately, he contracted pneumonia while in Germany and had to return home. His health continued to decline and on November 23, 1910, he passed away. As soon as Wilbur received the news he left for the funeral in Chicago.

Undoubtedly, Wilbur was saddened by the loss of his friend, but he also must have been relieved that they had resolved some of their differences before Chanute passed away. Chanute was nearly seventy-nine when he died.

CHAPTER TWENTY-NINE

LITIGATIONS AND EXHIBITIONS

On January 3, 1910, Judge Hazel of the Federal Circuit Court in Buffalo, New York, issued an injunction against the Herring-Curtiss Company. He concluded that the evidence presented in court supported the Wright brothers' claim of being the first ones to develop the information which they had patented.

That injunction restrained the Herring-Curtiss Company from manufacturing, selling or exhibiting aeroplanes, which forced the company to close. However, Glenn Curtiss immediately posted a bond of $10,000 and filed an appeal so that he could continue to conduct business. That was risky because, if the Court of Appeals upheld the Wrights' claim, he would have to pay the Wright Company a percentage of the money earned while the injunction was in effect.

Foreign aviators performing in the United States were similarly infringing on the Wrights' patent claims. The Wrights filed suit against the French aviator, Louis Paulham, one of the stars of the Reims races. He was scheduled in fly at Dominguez Field in Los Angeles, but was served an injunction as soon as he arrived on United States soil. He posted a bond and continued on tour. After earning $20,000 he returned to France. Claude Grahame-White, an English pilot, was also sued. He earned $100,000 while on tour in the United States and had to pay the Wright Company $1,700 for his infringement on the Wright patent.

When the suit was filed against the Herring-Curtiss Company in August of 1909, its board of directors called for Herring's patents. When he failed to comply, they obtained a court order requiring him to produce them. He couldn't, because there never had been any patents; they were simply a figment of his lively imagination. Herring and his lawyer both skipped town and Herring went into hiding for several months. The Herring-Curtiss Company floundered and finally declared bankruptcy on April 10, 1910.

Howard reports that:

> On June 14, 1910, less than six months later, the bond was returned and Judge Hazel's injunction was vacated by the U.S. Circuit Court of Appeals on the grounds that the infringement had not been clearly enough established to justify the granting of an injunction (Howard 332).

Not only were the Wrights' patents being infringed on in America but also in Europe. The French Wright Company brought a suit against the French offenders in late 1910. Wilbur traveled to France to testify before the Third Civil Tribunal. The state's attorney declared that the Wrights deserved recognition for the invention of the aeroplane but their patent application was invalid because of

Chanute's 1903 lecture before the Aero Club of France and the publication of Wilbur's first speech before the Western Society of Engineers. However, the judges ruled in favor of the Wrights, but then established a panel of aeronautical experts to determine if any of the "key elements of the Wright patent had been anticipated by other aeronautical pioneers." The defendants delayed the case by a variety of means until the Wrights' French patents ran out in 1917.

In Germany the Patent Office declared the Wright patent invalid because of prior disclosure. They cited Chanute's speech and Wilbur's lecture to the Western Society of Engineers. The case was appealed to the Imperial Supreme court, which Crouch says upheld the ruling (Crouch, p 417).

The Wrights negotiated an agreement with the Aero Club of America. Competitors were allowed to fly their infringing machines in meets sponsored by the club without any legal consequences.

One bright spot in 1910 was the presentation to the Wright brothers of the Langley Medal by the Smithsonian Institute. Charles D. Walcott, secretary of the Smithsonian, had established the Langley Medal to commemorate the aeronautical work of Samuel P. Langley, the former secretary who had built the ill-fated Aerodrome. The medal was to be given to acknowledge the work of those making a significant contribution to the field of aeronautics. The Wrights received the medal for "achievement in aerodynamic investigation and its application to aviation" (Howard 335). In his gracious acceptance speech, Wilbur urged the institution to encourage individuals involved in aerial experiments. Jakab and Young in *The Published Writings of Wilbur and Orville Wright* remarked:

> [The] 1910 Smithsonian annual report printed (on page 23) a statement which was attributed to Wilbur Wright and that was made to appear to be part of his remarks given at the presentation of the Langley medal. The statement gave the misleading impression that the Wrights credited Langley with a critical role in their success. This falsified quotation, paraphrased from a 1906 letter from Wilbur to Chanute commenting on Langley's death, was later used by the Wrights' opponents to undermine their standing as the true inventors of the airplane (37).

That report would later be cited by Orville as one of the areas of disagreement between the Smithsonian and the Wright bothers.

The brothers had divided their set of responsibilities. Wilbur became involved with the defense of their patent rights while Orville was occupied with the production of the Wright planes. In November 1910, a new factory opened on Home Road in Dayton. It produced two planes a month. However, the demand for planes was very limited and the Wrights ventured into a new area.

Several years earlier Chanute had urged them to enter the exhibition business. At that time, they had been reluctant to do so, but with so limited a demand for planes they realized that exhibition flying had possibilities. They contacted a veteran exhibition performer, Roy Knabenshue of Toledo, Ohio. Knabenshue had been in the exhibition business since 1904 when he had flown Tom Baldwin's airship, the *California Arrow,* at the 1904 St. Louis Exposition. The Wrights hired Knabenshue to set up and manage the exhibition business for them.

A training field for pilots was needed and Montgomery, Alabama, was chosen because of its warm weather. The first trainees were Walter Brookins, a man the Wrights had known since he was four years old, Arthur Welsh of Washington, D.C., Arch Hoxsey from Pasadena, California, and J.W. Davis of Colorado Springs, Colorado, who didn't fly, but became the team's handy man.

PILOTS IN TRAINING AT MONTGOMERY, ALABAMA, 1910

In May 1910, Huffman Prairie was leased for a training field and Orville and Brookins began training a new group of pilots there. Although it was renamed Simms Station, the same hummocks remained as in 1905 and the pilots still had to chase the horses and cows off the field so they could practice. The Dayton team consisted of Frank Coffin, Phil Parmalee, J. Clifford Turpin, Duval La Chapell and Ralph Johnstone of Kansas City, Missouri, a stunt bicyclist.

With the Simms Station field available, other members of the Wright family were able to experience the joys of flight. Eighty-one year-old Bishop Wright enjoyed his first plane ride in the passenger seat beside Orville. He seems to have been delighted by the experience and kept yelling, "Higher, Orville, higher." From then on he made many diary notations about flying events. Brother Lorin received his first ride on May 21. The Wrights' faithful mechanic, Charlie Taylor, who had worked hundreds of hours on aeroplane motors, had never ridden in a plane until May, 1910. The Wright brothers had made an agreement never to ride together in order to insure that one brother would survive in case there ever was a fatal accident. The only time they ever flew together was in the spring of 1910, at Huffman field.

Bishop Wright recorded in his diary his description of Orville's flight over the city of Dayton on Aviation Day, September 22, 1910. He wrote:

> Orville flew to Dayton, and back to Simms. At 5:00, Orville comes on his flyer, about 2,000 feet high, turns at Williams Street, goes near our home, flies along Third Street to the limits of the city, and rising to about 4,000 feet, goes up Mad River to their grounds. Came nine miles in ten minutes, returned slower. Many thousands see him (Papers 2: 999).

In June, 1910, at the Indianapolis Speedway, the brothers had a heart-stopping experience when Walter Brookins set a new altitude record of almost 6,000 feet but had engine failure on his descent, missed landing at the speedway and vanished from sight. The brothers found him about a quarter mile away standing beside his undamaged Flyer, calmly smoking a cigarette.

But Brookins luck didn't last. In August he swerved to miss a group of photographers when a gust of wind caught the Flyer and flipped it over backward, injuring Brookins and some spectators. Brookins sustained a broken nose, a broken ankle and several broken teeth. With Brookins out of commission, Arch Hoxsey and Ralph Johnstone became the stars of the team. Their fearless performances earned them the title of the Star Dust Twins.

The Wrights were always trying to improve the performance of their machines. Orville had noted earlier that the rudder being in the front caused some of the difficulties with the Flyer's performance. After a series of changes, the Wrights eliminated the front rudder altogether. The new machine was called the headless Flyer for a time but then simply Model B.

The Model B was built for distance and endurance and took many of the prizes at the Boston Squantum Meadows meet in September, 1910. President Theodore Roosevelt rode in an aeroplane for the first time with a Wright pilot, Arch Hoxsey, at an air show in St. Louis.

The Wrights were never keen on exhibition flying. When their pilots began having accidents, safety became the Wrights' major focus.

Each team member had his specialty. Brookins flew circles at an eighty-degree angle low to the ground. Johnstone was expert at steep dives and Dutch rolls. Hoxsey was the master of the Dive of Death, pulling out of a daring dive just in time to avoid crashing.

As the crowds grew hungrier for more daring stunts, the aviators took more chances. When Hoxsey swerved and hit a group of people injuring several, Wilbur drew the line. He wrote the following instructions to the team:

> I am much in earnest when I say that I want no stunts and spectacular frills put on the flights there. If each of you can make a plain flight of ten to fifteen minutes each day always keeping within the inner fence wall away from the grandstand and never more than three hundred feet high it will be just what we want. Under no circumstances make more than one flight each day apiece. Anything beyond plain flying will be chalked up as a fault and not as a credit (Howard 356).

Several European aviators had been killed by the time that the International Aviation Tournament opened at Belmont racetrack in October, 1910, but no American pilots had died as a result of a crash at that time.

The Wrights were primed to win the Bennett trophy. A special adaptation of the Model B was built. It was called the Baby Grand and had a wingspan of only twenty-one feet. The motor was eight cylinders and the plane attained 50-60 miles per hour. Orville flew a test flight, which was clocked at 70 miles per hour. Brookins was scheduled to fly for the trophy on Saturday. But when Brookins was making a trial run, four of the cylinders ceased firing and the plane hurtled to the ground. The skids were crushed and Brookins was injured.

The team's first fatality took place in Denver. Johnstone attempted to make a spiral glide when his machine went into a perpendicular dive. He was killed on impact. Arch Hoxsey was on Dominguez Field in Los Angeles when he was killed making a spiral dive after a gust of wind flipped the plane and it somersaulted to earth. The Wrights withdrew from the exhibition business in November 1911.

The commercial use of the aeroplane had already begun. In November, 1910, Phil Parmalee flew the first aerial freight delivery from Dayton to Columbus, Ohio. He carried a bolt of silk strapped to the passenger seat for the Morehouse-Martins Department Store. The store made a profit of $1,000 by selling swatches of silk.

Soon the owners of large city newspapers began to sponsor flying contests. A $10,000 prize was offered for the first round trip flight between Philadelphia and New York. Then a $25,000 prize was established for a flight between New York and Chicago. William Randolph Hearst presented a $50,000 prize for a coast-to-coast flight to be completed in thirty days or less.

The Armour Packing Company recognized the value of using the aeroplane in an advertising campaign. It had just developed a new grape soda, Vin Fizz, which it needed to promote. So, the company sponsored Cal Rogers, a Wright trained pilot, in his cross-country flight to win the Hearst prize. He needed to complete his flight within a month. Rodgers purchased a single-seat biplane with a thirty-two foot wingspan and a motor which produced 55 miles per hour.

VIN FIZZ was painted in large letters across the bottom of the lower wing. Rodgers hired Charlie Taylor as his mechanic. Charlie rode in the three-car support train, provided by the Armour Company. Rodgers had eleven major accidents during his cross-country flight. The first one took place just minutes after his take-off from New York when he flew under some telegraph wires and into a chicken coop.

The Vin Fizz, as it came to be called, was totaled and rebuilt several times before Rodgers made it to the shore of the Pacific Ocean. His beleaguered journey lasted twelve weeks instead of the month required to earn the prize. Five months after his historic flight ended, Rodgers was killed trying to avoid flying into a flock of gulls.

As Wilbur had stated in his acceptance speech at the Smithsonian, both he and Orville wanted to be able to return to their aeronautical investigations and experimenting. But that was not to be.

CHAPTER THIRTY

A TERRIBLE TOLL

In March 1911, Wilbur had gone to Europe to testify in the European infringement suits. The stress produced by those suits contributed to his succumbing to a very bad cold. It seemed to linger on despite the attentive care given him by Comtisse de Lambert, the wife of Count Charles de Lambert, a French pilot Wilbur had trained.

On March 28, Wilbur wrote his father about one of the medicines given him:

> The last one is a preparation of Dr. Doyen, a very celebrated Paris physician, and has a very interesting lot of pictures of microbes on the outside of the bottle. The story that goes with it is that the blood contains both good and bad microbes. Instead of attacking the bad microbes directly this medicine is supposed to incite the good microbes to jump onto the bad ones and destroy them. Stripped of all technical verbiage and fancy pictures the stuff seems to be merely a tonic in plain English (Kelly, 383).

Wilbur was weary with the business side of their operation and wrote Orville that the only reasons he was remaining in business at all was because of the responsibility he felt to their investors and because he didn't want a "lot of scoundrels" stealing their patents.

The Wrights were so occupied with obtaining the government contracts, the formation of commercial companies and with the patent infringement suits, that they had been unable to finish a project they had begun in 1906, the invention of an automatic stabilizer. The three axes of control system, which they developed in their 1903 plane put all the responsibility of maintaining the equilibrium of the machine in the hands of the pilot. Any small deviation could lead to disastrous results. The Wrights planned to develop a system which relieved the pilot of the task "of adjusting rudder, elevator and ailerons [. . .] for every irregularity of air movement in straightway flight" (Howard 367). Orville had finally perfected the mechanism and it was ready for testing but the patent, which had been applied for in 1908, had not yet been granted. The brothers decided to test it in Kitty Hawk, where they hoped they could test in secret.

Although Wilbur had returned from testifying in the patent suit in Europe, his testimony was needed in the Curtiss case, which meant Orville had to test the new device without the help of his older brother. Alexander Ogilvie, an English pilot who had purchased a Wright plane, came from England to help with the testing. Both brothers felt Ogilvie could be trusted to keep their new invention secret. A new glider was built in which the pilot sat upright and the elevator was in the rear.

Besides Alex Ogilvie, Orville was accompanied by his brother, Lorin, and Lorin's ten-year-old son, Buster. They arrived at the Wright camp on October 10, 1911. The high winds had done their usual damage to the buildings but they were repaired quickly and the group spent a couple days fishing and exploring the sounds of the Outer Banks.

When Orville went to pick up the crates with the new glider on October 13, he found four newsmen had also arrived. Among the group was Bruce Salley, the same reporter from Norfolk who had written several stories about the Wrights' 1908 flights on the Outer Banks.

Recognizing that there was no way to maintain secrecy, Orville and Ogilvie decided to spend the time gliding instead of testing. Both men made several spectacular flights as well as had several spectacular accidents. About a hundred glides were conducted. In one glide a whirlwind caught the glider that Orville was flying and turned it around smashing it into a sand dune. The longest glide was nine minutes and forty-five seconds. It was a world record that stood for ten years.

After the group broke camp they traveled back to the mainland on the *Hattie Creef,* accompanied by several of the newsmen. Aycock Brown, in his *The Birth of Aviation,* gave their names as John Mitchell and Van Ness Hardwood of the Associated Press, Mitchell of the New York *Herald,* and Arnold Kruchman and the photographer, Vargas, from the Hearst papers.

ORVILLE WRIGHT AND THE REPORTERS

The automatic stabilizer was finally patented in 1913. On December 31, 1913, Orville tested it at Huffman Prairie before a large crowd. He flew laps around the field with his hands held high in the air. The new device worked perfectly.

When the Wrights failed to purchase the services of Albert Zahm as an expert witness in the Wright vs. Curtiss case, Zahm did his best to discredit them, both in his court testimony and in his professional writing. In *Aerial Navigation,* Zahm claimed that any inventor could have patented the Wrights' system of wing warping and ailerons. He wrote, "it has been patented in one form or another by many practical aviators, some endeavoring to claim the whole contrivance, others claiming more restricted devices" (Howard 378).

On April 6, 1912, Wilbur wrote to E.C. Huffaker:

It is rather amusing, after having been called fools and fakers for six or eight years, to find now that people knew exactly how to fly all the time. People who had not the least idea of flying until within the last year or two now attempt to write books stating what the situation of the flying problems was in 1900 and 1901, when we made our first experiments in Kitty Hawk. In view of our experiments in 1901 it is amusing to hear them tell that the science of aerodynamics had been reduced to a very exact basis, so that anyone could calculate without difficulty the lift and drift of aeroplane surfaces. After the real truth had been discovered, old experiments seemed to have an importance in value sometimes, which they did not have at the time (Papers 2: 1041).

Wilbur was not in the least amused by Albert Zahm's attempt to discredit their work. He was determined to set the record straight. He wrote three articles for the *Aero Club of America Bulletin.*

While he was in France, Wilbur had personally inspected Clement Ader'a flying machine, the *Avion,* which was on display at a Paris museum. In fact during the patent suit the whole court had adjourned to the museum to view the craft and to hear Ader's testimony. In explaining his system of mastering equilibrium, which the defendants said was equivalent to the Wrights wing warping, Ader said he simply ran one propeller faster than the other propeller, which had the same result as wing warping. After his own inspection of Ader's machine, Wilbur concluded that the whole machine was ridiculous.

Another pioneer of flight, which infringers used to refute the Wrights' claim, was Louis Pierre-Mouillard. Judge Hand in the Wright Company vs. Louis Paulham suit ruled there was nothing in the nineteen claims that foreshadowed the Wrights' wing warping system. Mouillard's book, *The Empire the Air,* was one of the aeronautical classics, which so inspired the Wright brothers that they took up the pursuit of human flight. Jakab and Young in *The Published Writings of Wilbur and Orville Wright* remarked:

[The] 1910 Smithsonian annual report printed (on page 23) a statement which was attributed to Wilbur Wright and that was made to appear to be part of his remarks given at the presentation of the Langley medal. The statement gave the misleading impression that the Wrights credited Langley with a critical role in their success. This falsified quotation, paraphrased from a 1906 letter from Wilbur to Chanute commenting on Langley's death, was later used by the Wrights' opponents to undermine their standing as the true inventors of the airplane (37).

In the spring of 1912, Wilbur wrote "Otto Lilienthal " in the *Aero Club of America Bulletin*. Although the use of Lilienthal's air pressure tables had lead to considerable difficulties during the Wrights' glider experiments, they had provided a starting point from which a more accurate set of tables would be constructed. It was their questioning of the accuracy of Lilienthal's tables that led to their wind tunnel experiments from which the solution for human flight finally emerged. Wilbur admits in his article that Lilienthal had contributed more to the solution of human flight than any other nineteenth century pioneer of flight.

Wilbur traveled to Boston to consult with a Wright Company attorney on the Curtiss trial. After eating seafood at the hotel he became ill. He was still weak when he returned to Dayton but he continued to work.

The brothers had purchased seventeen acres of land in Oakwood and were planning a new house. The whole family (Bishop Wright, Katharine, Orville and Wilbur) went to the site on Thursday, May 2, 1912. Later in the afternoon the two brothers went to Simms Station to test a new model, Model C, for the army.

Wilbur was so ill by Saturday that Katharine insisted on calling the family doctor, Dr. Conklin. The good doctor ordered Wilbur to bed. On May 10, Wilbur sent for the attorney, Ezra Kuhns, and dictated his will which his secretary, Mabel Beck transcribed. Dr. Conklin had told Orville on May 16 it was safe for him to go to Washington to deliver the Model C to the army. When Wilbur learned Orville had left, he became so upset he had to be sedated.

It was not until Monday, May 20 that the doctors, Dr. Conklin and Dr. Spitler, said that Wilbur was very ill. Bishop Wright recorded every day in his diary. Wilbur seemed to improve, then he regressed. Finally on Thursday, May 30, 1912, Wilbur Wright breathed his last at 3:15 a.m. He was forty-five years old. Medically, he was a victim of typhoid fever but in reality, he was so worn down by the struggles of trying to protect their patent rights that his immune system just couldn't cope with the constant pressure he was under.

In his diary Bishop Wright wrote:

short life, full of consequences. An unfailing intellect, imperturbable temper, great self-reliance, and as great modesty, seeing the right clearly, pursuing it steadily, he lived and died (Papers 2:, 1046).

At the end of the year the father wrote the following testimony about his departed son:

In memory and intellect, there was none like him. He systemized everything. His wit was quick and keen. He could say or write anything he wanted to. He was not very talkative. His temper could hardly be stirred. He wrote much. He could deliver a fine speech, but was modest (Papers 2: 1046).

In his will Wilbur gives his own testimony to his father and Orville. He thanked his father "for his example of a courageous and upright life, and for his earnest sympathy with everything tending to my true welfare." Wilbur bequeathed $50,000 to each of his siblings (Katharine, Lorin and Reuchlin) and

$1,000 to his father for his little pleasures. Wilbur knew Katharine and Orville would provide for his father's needs. He left the remainder of his estate to Orville:

> who has been associated with me in all hopes and labors both of childhood and manhood, who, I am sure will use the property in very much the same manner as we would use it together in case we would both survive until old age (Howard 384).

Although Orville was devastated at the death of Wilbur he attempted to carry on, setting up an English company, filling the army contracts, conferring with attorneys over the patent suits and answering correspondence, but Orville really didn't have the heart for business and the maneuvering that was required.

WILBUR WRIGHT

CHAPTER THIRTY-ONE

A FIRM STAND

Less than two weeks after Wilbur's death, Orville suffered another devastating blow. Art Welsh and Lieutenant Leighton Hazelhurst died in the new Model C Flyer, which had been designed for the army. A.L. Welsh had been in the first group of pilots Orville trained in Montgomery, Alabama, in 1910 and was a member of the Wright exhibition team and an instructor at Huffman Prairie. Katharine and Orville went immediately to Washington, D. C., to attend their funerals.

Orville had been working on the automatic stabilizer, but had not yet tested it in public. He was very concerned about the army's planes "stalling" and continued to make efforts to overcome that difficulty. On November 16, 1912, he wrote Captain Charles DeForest Chandler:

Before the receipt of your letter, while working on the design for a fuselage machine for the Army, I had tried to devise some way of overcoming this very feature, which is present in all flying machines at the present time. The cause of the trouble is apparent, but I find it no easy matter to design a machine that will eliminate this trouble without introducing some other undesirable features. It is for this very reason that the proposal for the enclosed military machine has not been submitted. We are endeavoring to get up a design that will be safer and better in other respects than the present machines (Papers 2:1051-1052).

In the letter Orville suggested that a meeting with one of the pilots would be helpful. He said that he would be willing to go to Washington once he had completed his business for the Curtiss trial in Buffalo. Orville also promised to finish the design of the new machine after his return to Dayton and to "push it vigorously until it [was] completed."

That sounds like a man who was concerned about the army accidents and was giving the matter serious consideration by attempting to correct the problem. In his letter, Orville acknowledged the design flaw and said that the tendency of flying machines to dive when "stalling" was present in every prominent machine with which he was acquainted. In December 1913, he tested the automatic stabilizer, which he had designed to relieve the pilot of needing to maintain absolute control. The system was designed to sense changes in altitude and activate the wing-warping and elevator controls to restore the equilibrium of the aeroplane.

Orville appeared to be doing his best to pick up where Wilbur had left off. In February, he and Katharine traveled to England for the formation of the British Wright Company. Afterward they went to Berlin for a court hearing before the German Supreme Court. The court upheld the Patent Office ruling which acknowledged that the Wrights were the inventors of wing-warping, but denied them the right to an exclusive patent because of the prior public disclosure in Chanute's 1903 speech to the Aero Club of France and in Wilbur's speech to the Western Society of Engineers.

The situation in France wasn't much better. The French court ruled in favor of the Wrights, but it seemed that the owners of the infringing French machines intended to keep the case alive until the patent expired in 1917.

Katharine and Orville returned home only to find themselves confronting a major natural disaster. There was little rejoicing on Easter Sunday, March 23, 1913. Heavy rains had begun to fall and soon there was grave concern about the possibility of severe flooding. Dayton was at the crossroads of four waterways: the Miami, Stillwater, and Mad Rivers and Wolf Creek. The city had already experienced six major floods. The Miami River rose at the rate of six inches an hour. When Katharine and Orville left Tuesday morning for a meeting across town, they had no idea that upriver the Loramie Reservoir Dam had broken. Water swept south past the cities of Sidney, Piqua and Troy and into Dayton. The Miami River and Wolf Creek surrounded low-lying West Dayton, which was caught in the deluge. When the Stafford Avenue levee was breached, Katharine and Orville were unable to return home. All the telephones were out of commission and they were unable to contact their father, Bishop Wright. They had no way of knowing that the elderly bishop had been rescued by canoe and was safe on Williams Street. They posted notices asking for his whereabouts. The following day they learned he was safe.

Orville was concerned for the safety of his historic photographic glass negatives and the 1903 Flyer, which were stored in a shed behind the Hawthorne Street home. Other important documents of the Wright brothers' progress were stored on the second floor of the bicycle shop on Third Street. Both areas of the city were under siege from the raging floodwaters. Hawthorne Street was covered by eight feet of water. Third Street was totally flooded and, to make matter worse, a broken gas main fueled fires throughout the area. Most buildings in the business area caught fire. The bicycle shop was spared the fire, but not the flood, which filled the first floor with twelve feet of muddy water.

When the floodwaters finally receded three days later, it was learned that three hundred and seventy-one lives were lost and the property damage was estimated at one hundred million dollars. The Wrights were one of the more fortunate families; their loss amounted to about five thousand dollars. Most of the family furniture downstairs was lost. Unfortunately the priceless negatives were damaged, but the 1903 Flyer, which had remained in its wooden packing crates, was not, even though the wooden crates were under many feet of mud.

That historic bit of wood and cloth eventually became a source of controversy between the prestigious Smithsonian Institute and Orville Wright. The seeds of this disagreement had begun several years before Wilbur's death and would not finally be resolved until 1948, a year after Orville's death.

Wilbur had been the businessman in the family, not Orville, but in order to proceed with the patent suits, Orville had to maintain his financial resources. That meant succeeding Wilbur as president of the Wright Company. That position as president of the company gave Orville the control he needed to fire the factory manager, Frank Russell, whom neither he or Wilbur had liked and who had been hired by the Wright Company board. In July 1913, he hired Grover Loening. Loening had introduced himself to Wilbur during the Hudson-Fulton Celebration while he was still a college student at Columbia University. He was the first person to graduate from a university with an engineering degree in aeronautics.

Orville treated Loening much like a younger brother. He enjoyed verbally sparring with him just as he and Wilbur had done. Loening liked Orville; however, he was frustrated by what he thought was a lack of drive and business acuity.

What Loening perceived as a man lacking initiative was a man depressed by the loss of his closest companion, his brother, Wilbur, a man in constant pain from several undiagnosed hip fractures, a man under the pressure of preparing court testimony and a man adjusting to the demands of a corporate board.

Orville was determined to win the patent suit because he was convinced, rightly so, that the demands of the patent suits had so weakened Wilbur's physical system that he had no strength left to resist the progression of typhoid fever. Bishop Wright's diary entries support this conclusion. He wrote that Wilbur was so emotionally and physically exhausted after meeting with the company attorneys that he returned home drained of all color.

Loening was upset because Orville refused to change the basic Wright design; however, Orville was reluctant to change the design before the patent suits were settled. He thought that changing the design could be interpreted as an admission that the Wright design was deficient.

Other flying machine models began to dominate the field and the Curtiss machine became an army standard. But both the Curtiss machine and the Wright Model C were responsible for several army officers' deaths. Loening said the problem was a design flaw. Orville felt the design was partly to blame, but so was pilot error. He designed an angle of incidence indicator which warned the pilot if his climb or dive became too steep.

Then on December 31, 1913, he made his first public demonstration of the automatic stabilizer before the members of the Aero Club of America at Huffman Field. He circled the field seven times with his hands off the controls in order to demonstrate the effectiveness of his invention. On February 5, 1914, Orville was awarded the Collier trophy for the most significant contribution to aeronautics during 1913. However, Orville's model was soon out-distanced by Lawrence Sperry's model, which used gyroscopes and became the basis of all future automatic stability systems.

Finally in January 1914, the United States Circuit Court sustained Judge Hazel's decision in which he had declared that ailerons were the equivalent of wing warping. In the end, the Wright patent was acknowledged as valid and Glenn Curtiss and company were found guilty of infringing on the Wright patent.

What happened next was a complete surprise to Grover Loening and the Wright Company board of directors who thought that the court decision provided the perfect opportunity to establish a monopoly and force Curtiss and other manufacturers out of business. Orville was not interested in creating a monopoly; what he wanted was to get rid of the New York capitalists on the board. He felt they intended to appoint as company attorney an associate of President Woodrow Wilson just so they could have some political advantage.

Orville deliberately infuriated his board by announcing that all aeroplane manufacturers except Curtiss were free to use the Wright patent as long as they paid a twenty per cent royalty on all the machines they produced. Loening said that, once the lawsuit was over, all Orville wanted was "tribute, royalties from everyone." Perhaps what Orville wanted was justice. In the article, "Are the Wrights Justified?," published in *Aeronautics* in April, 1910, the Wright brothers wrote:

> When a couple of flying machine inventors fish, metaphorically speaking, in waters where hundreds had previously fished for thousands of years in vain, and after risking their lives hundreds of times, and spending years of time and thousands of dollars, finally succeed in making a catch, there are people who think it a pity that the courts should give orders that the rights of the inventors shall be respected and that those who wish to enjoy the feast shall contribute something to pay the fishers (Howard 333).

It is inaccurate to say that all Orville wanted was tribute; what he wanted is what all people want, what all people are entitled to, fair treatment. However, he was not going to get that from the Curtiss associates. Curtiss was already trying to circumvent the court decision. He tried using only one aileron at a time, thinking that put him outside the Wright patent. But that was covered in Claim One of the patent even though it had not been cited in court. This provided grounds for a new lawsuit. Orville was furious, but he refused to take action. This further outraged his board.

The company had a more serious problem. On February 9, 1914, another army pilot died in a crash. The army wanted answers. Orville sent Oscar Brindly to investigate. He found that part of the problem was poor maintenance. Major Samuel Reber, the officer in charge of army aviation, advertised for an engineer to oversee the care of the flyers.

Grover Loening had been dissatisfied with Orville's apparent lack of ambition and applied for the job. Once he was hired by the army, he declared all the Wright and Curtiss pusher models (models with rear propellers) unsafe. He then rebuilt a Burgess tractor flying machine and incorporated all the latest European innovations in it.

CHAPTER THIRTY-TWO

THE AERODROME AFFAIR

Curtiss had decided on a new tactic. If he could prove that the Langley Aerodrome had been capable of flight, he might win in another lawsuit with the Wright Company. Dr. Charles Walcott, the new director of the Smithsonian, had worked under Langley and was devoted to honoring his memory. In his zeal to preserve the reputation of his former boss, Walcott planned to establish an aeronautics exhibit. The Aerodrome motor was already on display and Dr. Walcott planned on hanging the Aerodrome in one of the great halls.

In 1910, Walcott wrote the Wrights requesting one of their machines "to illustrate two very important steps in the history of aeronautical art." In his reply, Wilbur had offered to "reconstruct the 1903 Wright Flyer with which the first flights were made at Kitty Hawk," and even indicated space which would be needed to accommodate it. Dr. Walcott ignored their offer and instead requested the 1908 military Flyer that had attracted worldwide attention and models of other Wright planes. These were to be exhibited with the Langley Aerodrome. The Wrights felt that exhibiting the 1908 military model next to the Aerodrome would give the public the impression that the Aerodrome had been capable of flight in 1903 and it was only in 1909 that the Wrights were successful in achieving flight. They felt the Smithsonian was trying to create a false perception of what happened and didn't respond to this request. It was only when the new buildings of the Massachusetts Institute of Technology were dedicated and Alexander Graham Bell saw the 1903 Wright Flyer on exhibit that the matter was reopened years later.

Obviously, the failure of the Aerodrome was a sensitive issue with Walcott. In 1898, Dr. Walcott, then director of the U.S. Geological Survey, had persuaded the officials at the War Department to support Langley's aeronautical research. Langley had been given $50,000 for his research.

After the U.S. Circuit Court decision in January of 1914, an associate of Curtiss contacted the Smithsonian and requested the use of the Langley's Aerodrome, with the intention of rebuilding and flying it. Alexander Graham Bell, a regent, and the administrator, Dr. Rathbun, advised Dr. Walcott against loaning the Aerodrome to Lincoln Beachey, the Curtiss associate.

But when Curtiss made the same request, Walcott agreed and then spent two thousand dollars of the Smithsonian's funds to support the project plus the services of Dr. Albert Zahm, then head of the Langley Laboratory. Zahm had been the "expert" recommended to Walcott by Octave Chanute. He was also the technical aeronautics witness on the Curtiss defense team.

To indicate that this was an unbiased research project was a complete distortion of the reality. Zahm couched his explanation in the 1914 Smithsonian *Annual Report* as follows:

> The main objects of these renewed trials were first to show whether the original Langley machine was capable of sustained free flight with a pilot, and secondly, to determine more fully the advantages of the tandem wing type of aeroplane.

The true motives were quite transparent. Curtiss wanted ammunition to use in the next lawsuit. If he could demonstrate that the Aerodrome had been capable of flight in early December 1903, he would have it. Walcott wanted to vindicate the reputation of Samuel Langley, who had been ostracized by both the professional community and the public for the failure of the Aerodrome and the loss of the $50,000 of public funds spent on the project. Albert Zahm wanted revenge for his perceived slight from the Wrights when they failed to purchase his services as an expert witness and because he had been embarrassed when Wilbur pointed out inconsistencies in his court testimony.

What happened next should have been an embarrassment to the prestigious Smithsonian Institution. The fact that it was not shows just how blinded Dr. Walcott was by his desire to restore the reputation of Samuel Langley. Their published goal was to restore the Aerodrome to its original condition in 1903. However, they went far beyond that and substantially improved the aircraft.

> Three fundamental changes were made in the design of the wings themselves: (1) The camber was greatly changed; (2) the shape of the leading edge was entirely different; (3) the aspect ratio--the ratio of span to chord—was increased. These three features are the most important characteristics in determining the efficiency of a wing. The change of the camber of itself may increase the efficiency of a wing by thirty percent. And not only were the wings changed as to design, but they were strengthened by various means of reinforcing and trussing not used by Langley. Even the cloth on the wings was improved by varnishing, to make the wings more efficient. Langley had not used varnish on the cloth.

(Kelly 312)

The fact that the craft was fitted with floats and launched from the water can be excused as a matter of safety. After a brief trial, the machine was refitted with a Curtiss engine and other changes made. When the results of these tests were published in the 1914 Smithsonian *Annual Report,* Albert Zahm wrote that the Aerodrome:

> with its original structure and power, is capable of flying with a pilot and several hundred pounds of useful load. It is the first aeroplane in history of which this can truthfully be said. [. . .] The Langley aeroplane, without floats, restored to its original condition and provided with stronger bearings, should be able to carry a man and sufficient supplies for a voyage lasting practically the whole day.

These exaggerated claims were published for several continuous years in the *Annual Report*. When the Aerodrome was returned to the Smithsonian, it was once again "restored to its original condition" and displayed in the Arts and

Industries Building. It was labeled "the first aeroplane in the history of the world capable of sustained free flight" (Kelly 311).

Orville was understandably upset. He had documented proof that the Aerodrome had been altered. Griffith Brewer, the first Englishman to fly and a staunch supporter of the Wrights, had visited Hammondsport and taken pictures of alterations being made. He had gathered information documenting the changes which were already completed. The following year Lorin, Orville's older brother, had traveled to Hammonsport and saw one of the flights of the renovated craft in which its wings folded up. Orville was furious.

During the period that this conspiracy was being carried out, Orville had been involved in his own maneuvering. In the spring of 1914, he began to buy up the shares held by the Wright Company board members. Most of his own money was tied up in company capital and he was forced to borrow money for the first time in his life. The only board member whose stock he didn't acquire was that of his friend, Robert Collier. Orville guaranteed a hundred percent profit on each man's investment.

Once Orville had total control of the company, he sprang into action. In November 1914, he filed a new lawsuit against the Curtiss Aeroplane and Motor Company. He then prepared the necessary court depositions and filed for a new patent, which incorporated all the changes made in the Flyer since the 1906 patent was granted. Finally, he put the Wright Company up for sale. On October 15, 1915, Orville Wright sold the Wright Company to a group of New York financiers. It was rumored that he received 1.5 million dollars plus a contract of $25,000 to be the consulting engineer. After repaying all his loans Orville was finally free to pursue his own experiments. In the end, he proved himself a better businessman than anyone ever imagined.

THE WRIGHT FAMILY AT HAWTHORNE HILL

CHAPTER THIRTY-THREE

FOLLOWING HIS HEART

Orville was finally free of all his business obligations and able to pursue his own interests. He built a laboratory at 15 North Broadway, about a block away from the bicycle shop in Dayton, Ohio. Over the next several decades it became his haven. It had a reception area and an office with a big rol-top desk in the front. His well-equipped laboratory was in the rear of the building.

For a while, Charlie Taylor came to work for him, but Charlie missed the camaraderie of the factory workers and returned to work at the Dayton-Wright Company. Mabel Beck, who had been Wilbur's faithful secretary, worked for Orville, typing his letters and keeping away unwanted visitors. She was such an effective gatekeeper that, at times, she terrified even Orville's family and friends.

Mabel and Katharine weren't particularly fond of each other. And Carrie Grumbach, Orville's housekeeper of many decades, refused to let Mabel in the Hawthorne mansion and even told Orville if that woman ever came in the front door she was going out the back. The animosity among the three women in Orville's life didn't seem to bother him, for each had her own unique place in his world.

ORVILLE'S LABORATORY

On March 10, 1917, Orville fell in love. The object of his affection was a small ball of fluff named Scipio after a Roman general. That sixteen-pound St. Bernard puppy grew to a whopping one hundred and sixty pounds and became Orville's constant companion from 1917 until 1923, when he passed away. Orville built a fence behind the laboratory so he could take his beloved pet to work with him.

Scipio even went on the family vacation to Lambert Island, Ontario, Canada. While there, he encountered a porcupine and had to be strapped to a wooden door to have the quills removed. That must have been an excruciatingly painful experience for both the dog and Orville. When Orville passed away in 1948, a picture of Scipio was found in his wallet. Orville Wright had great compassion for this giant canine who suffered from severe arthritis pain which was similar to the pains he endured.

ORVILLE'S DOG, SCIPIO

When the United States entered World War I in April 1917, Orville was commissioned as a major in the Aviation Section of the Signal Reserve Corps. He remained in Dayton and worked with the engineers of the Dayton-Wright Company, which was owned by four of his friends. The Dayton-Wright Company had incorporated five days after the United States declared war on Germany. Orville Wright had no financial interest in the company, but he allowed his friends to use his name in the company's title. (It was during this time period that the spelling of aeroplane was changed to airplane. Neither Orville nor Great Britain accepted the new spelling.)

One of the owners of the Dayton-Wright Company and a friend of Orville's, Edward Deeds, became a member of the Aircraft Production Board. He divested himself of any financial interests in the company when he became responsible for aircraft procurement. After the war there were investigations concerning Deeds' association with the company, but after much testimony no court action was ever taken.

Europe was far ahead in the production of the airplane, even though it had been an American invention. The need for warplanes was so enormous that the only solution seemed to be to use European models made in America and equipped with the American-built Liberty engine.

A British observation and bombing plane, the DeHavilland-4s, was sent to Dayton to be copied and constructed there. Drawings had to be prepared in order to accommodate the American-built engine. There were shortages of materials and strikes, which delayed production. On August 9, 1918, the first American-built DeHavilland-4s flew over the front lines. The war ended three months later.

Orville's contribution to the war effort had been to lend his name to the Dayton company and to consult with the engineers concerning the changes, which were made in redesigning the DH-4s. He also worked on a project for the Signal Corps, the Kettering Bug or aerial torpedo, an unmanned flying bomb. The Armistice was signed before the project was completed.

On May 13, 1918, Orville piloted a plane for the last time. He flew a 1911 Wright model alongside the first Dayton-built DH-4s. Orville's last technical contribution to aeronautics was the development of the split flap used to increase lift and reduce speed in a steep dive. He and James H. Jacobs designed, developed and patented it. The Navy Bureau of Aeronautics in 1922 felt it was useless but, twenty years later, it was used in the Douglas SBD Dauntless dive-bombers in the Pacific.

In 1920, President Wilson appointed Orville to the National Advisory Committee for Aeronautics (NACA), which was responsible for identifying research problems that could open the way for further aeronautical progress. The Langley Research Center at Hampton Roads, Virginia, was its first facility. Its discoveries enabled the United States airplane industry to become a world leader. Orville was a faithful member of the NACA for twenty-eight years. He also served on the Daniel and Florence Guggenheim Fund for the Promotion of Aeronautics. The Fund existed from 1926-1930 and was responsible for several important advances in aviation such as high-speed flight and rocket engine technology.

Orville was always interested in the small inventor and those seeking information. He often spent time doing research in order to give a helpful answer. Once when he was invited to go to his grandnephew's fraternity house at Ohio's Miami University, a student asked him to clarify something about aviation he had read in his textbook. Orville asked to see it. After reading the passage Orville said, "Oh, this is wrong." and wrote the correction in the margin. At the student's request, Orville added his initials.

Orville never ceased inventing or fiddling. The mansion on Hawthorne Hill was his creation. He had the firm of Schenck and Williams draw up the plans, but the design was his. He supervised every detail, planning the heating, plumbing and electrical systems. He piped in rainwater, which was collected in an underground cistern. He spent the rest of his life maintaining these three systems.

In the reception hall, Orville designed a special niche for the beautiful bronze sculpture that the Aero Club of France had given to him and Wilbur in 1908. He even created the exact color that he wanted for the woodwork, and he and Charley Grumbach painted the woodwork themselves.

HAWTHORNE HILL IN WINTER

He loved to read and maintained a varied selection of books. Some of the subjects were world and American history, aviation and children's literature. He also liked to read the *Journal of the Ohio and Archaeological Quarterly*. But he wasn't fond of holding a publication for long periods so he drilled holes in the arms of his chair in order to accommodate a book rest that he designed. Undoubtedly, he rivaled Thomas Jefferson in his homey inventiveness.

Hawthorne Hill was a gracious and unpretentious home. Orville's cousin, Jay R. Petree, said it had a feeling of quiet restfulness. Many prominent people visited there. In 1927, Charles Lindberg landed the *Spirit of St. Louis* at the Wright Field after his historical flight across the Atlantic. Orville and General William Gilmore, who were to take him to a parade in his honor, greeted him, but Lindberg wanted to avoid a public reception, so Orville drove him to Hawthorne Hill instead of to the parade. However it wasn't long before the crowds discovered Lindberg was at Orville's home. There was much pushing, shoving and trampling of the bushes and flowerbeds to get a glimpse of their new national hero. Finally, in order to avoid the complete destruction of the Hawthorne Hill grounds, Lindberg made a public appearance from the home's balcony. Some other distinguished guests to visit Hawthorne Hill were General William Mitchell,

Admiral Richard Byrd, Franklin Roosevelt, Alexander Graham Bell and Thomas A. Edison.

The Wright family had never taken a vacation before 1916. In the spring of that year, Orville thought it was time. He rented a cottage in Canada on Lake Huron's Georgia Bay. While touring the lake, he discovered Lambert Island, which he liked so much that he bought it. The island had seven buildings: a main house, three small cottages, a pump house, an icehouse house and a tool shed - just perfect for a man who loved to tinker.

Orville's ides of a vacation consisted of remodeling or moving the cabins, taking out and replacing docks and fussing with the pumping system. Clothes were washed with the aid of a pump powered by a Johnson motor and a steady stream of water from the lake. He designed a cart to haul ice and baggage up a steep hill to the cottages. Within a few years it became "Orville's Railroad" and ran on a set of wooden rails. He also designed a toaster that would produce a perfect piece of toast every time.

In his later years Orville displayed a temperament similar to his mother's. He became more introspective and less likely to initiate conversations with persons he didn't know. But he enjoyed a good conversation with friends and often talked late into the night.

Orville was totally devoted to his family and their welfare. His nieces and nephews became his family when Reuchlin and Lorin passed away. "Uncle Orv" loved to play practical jokes on his family and friends. Harold Miller, his niece's husband said the family enjoyed his teasing because they knew "he only teased those he cared for." He reported that it was easy to know when Orville was in a gleeful mood because, although he tried to hide gleeful intentions, the "twitch" of his mustache and the twinkle in his eyes gave him away. Once he tried to convince his friend, Griffith Brewer, that he had psychic powers by pretending to find a book, which contained a certain quotation, while he was blindfolded. Orville did find the book, only because he had pulled out the volume directly above it just enough to so he could find it while blindfolded.

In 1923 he designed a set of clowns called "Flips and Flops" to delight his grandnieces and nephews at Christmas time. Ivonette Wright-Miller, Orville's niece, described it as a contraption about eighteen inches long with a springboard at one end and a double trapeze at the other end. When a clown was released from the springboard, it flew through the air and caught the topside of the trapeze. Both children and adults were so charmed by the toy that Orville patented it and Harold Miller arranged to have the Miami Wood Specialty Company produce it.

Family was important to Orville but no one was closer to Orville than his sister, Katharine, who has been called the "First Lady of Flight." She had abandoned her own career as a high school Latin teacher when Orville most needed her after his accident in 1908 at Fort Myers. But Katharine had not been the loser; she had gained a whole new life. She traveled with Orville to Europe, where her knowledge of foreign languages and outgoing personality became a valuable asset to her two brothers as they attempted to market their invention. She met kings, prime ministers and presidents. She became part of their honorary presentations both in Europe and America.

It was Katharine who persuaded her brothers to build a more suitable home in which to receive the many important people who visited Dayton to see the Wright brothers. She helped with the selection of Hawthorne Hill in the Oakland section of Dayton. No doubt, she even influenced the Colonial Revival architectural style they choose. To furnish the completed home, she traveled to Grand Rapids, Michigan, with Orville and together they chose the furniture. Hawthorne Hill became her home as well as Orville's and she became its hostess, helping entertain the many dignitaries that came to visit.

Orville and Katharine were as close as any brother and sister could be. They had been together for most of their lives. Orville was convinced that that's the way it would remain. But then Katharine fell in love with a former college friend and fellow trustee of Oberlin College, Henry Joseph Haskell. Henry and his wife, Isabel, had been frequent visitors to the Wright home over the years. When Isabel passed away in 1923, Henry began to correspond with Katharine.

In time the two fell in love. Katharine avoided telling Orville for she knew he would be upset. And he was. In fact, he was so upset he wouldn't even attend her wedding at Oberlin College on November 20, 1926. When she moved to Kansas City where Henry was an editor of the *Kansas City Star,* Orville refused to have any contact with his sister. But in March, 1929, Katharine contracted a severe case of pneumonia and, at Lorin's insistence, Orville went to see her. He was with her when she died.

One can imagine the meeting was bittersweet for Orville. There must have been relief that the years of separation had ended, but also gut-wrenching sorrow when Katharine died. Her husband agreed to let her body return to Dayton where the funeral was held at Hawthorne Hill. She was buried at Woodland Cemetery in the family plot where her parents and Wilbur were buried. Bishop Wright had died on April 3, 1917, his wife, Susan, on July 4, 1889 and Wilbur on May 30, 1912. In time Orville would join them, but not for many more years.

For Orville, who was a man of principle, it must have been a puzzle when others claimed what was rightfully Wilbur's and his, the first manned power flight. But there always seemed to be another claimant or his supporters who thought otherwise. One such person was John Joseph Montgomery who claimed to have used wing warping for lateral control before the Wright brothers. After Montgomery's death, Victor Lougheed persuaded his heirs to bring suit against Orville. From that court case came Orville's wonderful, *How We Invented the Aeroplane,* his court deposition, edited by Fred Kelly. Another myth, which Orville had to contend with, was that of Gustave Whitehead. Stella Randolph had written an account of his purported flights in *The Lost Flights of Gustave Whitehead.* Orville countered with an article in *U. S. Air Services,* "The Mythical Whitehead Flight." Although the myth continued, the facts remain: the Wrights were the first to fly.

Orville's last big project was the restoration of the 1905 Flyer for the Deeds Carillon Park in 1947. Harvey Geyer, who had worked in the Wright plant from 1910 to 1912, volunteered to work on the reconstruction under Orville's watchful eye. Orville never lived to see the opening of the park, but he had made sure the Flyer's restoration was authentic in every detail.

Both Wilbur and Orville had hoped the aeroplane would be used to prevent war because of its scouting capability. In 1917, Orville told a reporter, "The nation with the most eyes will win and put an end to war. This is what we planned and this is what will happen" (Howard 416). He was so horrified by what actually happened he concluded: 'The aeroplane had made war so terrible that I do not believe any country will again care to start a war" (Howard 416).

During most of both world wars, Orville had tried to solve his own conflict with the Smithsonian Institute but to no avail. It remained unresolved after many decades.

CHAPTER THIRTY-FOUR

FINALLY

With World War I waging in Europe in 1917 and after the formation of the Manufacturers Aircraft Association, the patent wars were finally laid to rest. The government had called for a mandatory settlement to patent conflicts and for cross-licensing of patented technology. Patent holders who contributed their patents to the patent pool received compensation according to the patent's value. Members of the association paid a flat fee for the use of any and all patents in the pool.

Thus the defendants in the Curtiss patent suit never used their contrived results of the Langley Aerodrome tests in court. But the Smithsonian Institution's duplicity followed for several more decades. Its prestigious position meant its published findings went unquestioned and soon Dr. Langley was declared "Discoverer of the Air" by the *Literary Digest*.

Up until 1921, Orville was convinced that Dr. Walcott, secretary of the Smithsonian, was unaware of the structural changes made to the Aerodrome in Hammondsport by Curtiss and Albert Zahm. Griffith Brewer, Orville's long-time friend, went to the Wrights' defense. Brewer was the first Englishman to fly with Wilbur at Le Mans. He had been instrumental in setting up the contract with the Short brothers in England and in the establishment of the British Wright Company. As a representative of the British aeronautical community, he had visited Hammondsport and witnessed first hand some of the changes which were being made in the Aerodrome and had taken several pictures of the work being done.

On October 20, 1921, Brewer gave a lecture in England to the Royal Society of Arts which was entitled "Aviation's Greatest Controversy." He laid bare the evidence for all to see. One by one he revealed the changes made to the Aerodrome in Hammondsport and the erroneous information published by the Smithsonian. To those seeking the truth, the evidence was undeniable; the original Langley Aerodrome of 1903 was not capable of flight. What was tested at Hammondsport was not the same machine. It was a structurally reinforced version of the original machine equipped with a modified Langley motor using a magneto to jump-start the engine and an automobile-type carburetor with a float feed, these changes and others made any results questionable.

Public opinion changed and several articles were written decrying the farce, but the officials at the Smithsonian remained silent. Eventually, Dr. Walcott replied by appointing two members of the National Advisory Committee for Aeronautics who suggested a label change for the Aerodrome. The label read:

In the opinion of many competent to judge, this was the first heavier-than-air craft in the history of the world capable of sustained free flight under its own power, carrying a man (added later) "slightly antedated" the 1903 Wright machine (Howard 427).

Meanwhile, Orville was concerned about the condition of the Flyer. He wrote to Brewer in 1923 that he was worried about the danger of fire where it was stored, but at the time he had no better place for it. Brewer suggested sending the Flyer to England to be exhibited at the Science Museum in London. In answer to the many objections sent in letters protesting his decision, Orville wrote:

> I believe my course in sending our Kitty Hawk machine to a foreign museum is the only way of correcting the history of the flying-machine, which by false and misleading statements has been perverted by the Smithsonian Institution.
>
> In its campaign to discredit others in the flying art, the Smithsonian has issued scores of these false and misleading statements. They can be proved to be false and misleading from documents. But people of today do not take the trouble to examine this evidence.
>
> With this machine in any American museum the national pride would be satisfied; nothing further would be done and the Smithsonian would continue its propaganda. In a foreign museum this machine will be a constant reminder of the reason of its being there, and after the people and petty jealousies of this day are gone, the historians of the future may examine impartially the evidence and make history accord with it.
>
> Your regret that this old machine must leave our country can hardly be so great as my own (Kelly 315).

Still Orville waited. In 1925 he wrote Chief Justice William Howard Taft, then chancellor of the Smithsonian and asked him to have an impartial committee appointed which could review the evidence and make a judgment about the authenticity of the claims made after the Hammondsport testing.

Taft replied that his appointment was in name only and his present duties didn't allow him time to spend on a matter, which should be decided by the secretary of the Smithsonian Institution.

Any member of the Board of Regents could have called for an investigation, but none of them did. It should be noted that the board was made up of the vice president of the United States, the Chief Justice, three members of the Senate, three members of the House of Representatives and six private citizens. The fact that not one member of the board thought the matter important enough to warrant an investigation is unbelievable.

Still Orville waited. Finally in early 1928, seeing no hope for a resolution of the controversy in sight, he sent the Flyer to the Science Museum in South Kensington, London, England. The Flyer was to stay in England for a period of five years. It would only be returned if he personally wrote a letter requesting its return.

When Dr. Walcott died in 1927, the new Smithsonian secretary, Dr. Charles G. Abbott, invited Orville to Washington to discuss the situation. Orville agreed to bring the Flyer home only if the Smithsonian in its *Annual Report* corrected the misinformation published in its earlier reports. Dr. Abbott was in a quandary. He didn't want to damage the reputation of Dr. Walcott or the Smithsonian. He said it was impossible to determine what effects the changes had had on the performance of the Aerodrome. Orville, of course, knew better. He replied that if experts knew what changes had been made, they could determine the effects those changes had on the Aerodrome's performance. That argument fell on deaf ears.

Orville tried again in 1933. He wrote Dr. Abbott suggesting that an impartial panel be appointed to settle the question once and for all. Dr. Abbott agreed, but then he appointed a panel of three public officials, all of whom were members of the Smithsonian. Additionally, he prepared a list of questions to be answered by the panel. Most of the questions had little to do with the problem to be solved.

Orville tried to simplify the matter. He said all that was needed was to publish a paper listing in one column the features of the original 1903 Aerodrome and, in another parallel column, the features of the 1914 modified Aerodrome along with a statement which said that the Smithsonian had been misled by Dr. Albert Zahm's report on the results of the Hammondsport testing. Once again Dr. Abbott muddied the waters.

It wasn't until 1942 that finally, through the efforts of biographer Fred Kelly, a statement was prepared that met the approval of both men. Within the statement were two parallel columns listing the features of the original Aerodrome and the features of the 1914 modified Aerodrome. The statement was published by the Smithsonian on October 14, 1942 and is contained in Fred Kelly's *The Wright Brothers* on pages 324-333.

In a letter to Dr. Abbott Orville wrote :

I can well understand the difficult position you found yourself in when you took over the administration of the Institution at a time when it had on its hands an embarrassing controversy for which you were not responsible, so I appreciate the more your effort to correct the record of the tests at Hammondsport in 1914 which brought on that controversy (Howard 440).

Although the controversy between the Wrights and the Smithsonian was settled in 1942, the war between the Allies and Germany was raging. The precious Flyer had been stored underground to protect it from the German bombs raining down on London.

The fortieth anniversary of the first flight was celebrated in 1943. President Franklin D. Roosevelt invited Orville to attend a gala affair in Washington. In his letter of acceptance, Orville agreed to attend, but said, "his inabilities as a speaker compel [him] to decline a speaking part in the program" (Papers 2: 1174). Orville wrote that he would be pleased if the president would make the announcement regarding the return of the Flyer at the dinner that was planned. The presentation of the Collier trophy to General Hap Arnold for Air Force's participation in the progress of World War II was also scheduled for that same evening. Arnold had been one of the Wrights' student pilots.

President Roosevelt had just returned from conferences in Tehran and Northern Africa and was unable to attend the festivities. Orville reminded Jesse Jones, the Secretary of Commerce, who presided in the president's absence, that he only agreed to attend if he weren't asked to speak. His wish was apparently ignored, because Jones read the president's letter concluding with the words:

> In closing I can think of only one additional tribute to General Arnold, will you please ask Orville Wright, the great teacher, to act for me in handing the Collier trophy to General Arnold, the great student (Howard 440).

He handed the trophy to Orville. Orville was a man of his word. With the newsreel cameras rolling, he handed the trophy to General Arnold without uttering a single syllable.

The Wright Flyer was resurrected from its underground tomb in July, 1945. Orville had written Colonel Mackintosh, the director of the Science Museum, on December 8, 1943, requesting the Flyer's return when transportation would be less hazardous. He agreed that the Flyer could remain six months after the war ended so a copy could be made, but he wished to correct the drawings made by the draftsmen who had assumed that the Flyer was symmetrical, which it was not. Orville pointed out in his letter that the Flyer was four inches longer on the right side than on the left.

Orville did not live to see the Flyer installed in its place of honor at the Smithsonian. He had, however, seen several monuments erected in honor of the Wright brothers' magnificent achievement of manned flight.

In 1926, W. O. Saunders Elizabeth City, North Carolina, contacted Lindsay Warren, the representative from the First Congressional District to the House of Representatives concerning the erection of a memorial in Kill Devil Hills at the site of the first flight. Warren introduced a bill in the House while another bill was introduced in the Senate. On March 2, 1927, President Coolidge signed a $50,000 appropriations bill into law. With the signing of this bill the process for the establishment of a national monument to honor the Wright brothers began.

In eastern North Carolina Saunders was instrumental in the formation of the Kill Devil Hills Memorial Association, later known as the First Flight Society; as stated in their pamphlet, the goals of the organization were:

> to bridge Currituck Sound between the mainland and Kitty Hawk, and to build a hard surface road from Kitty Hawk to Kill Devil Hill; to make the proposed monument accessible to all Americans by motor. [. . .] [And to build] an airport and suitable accommodations for aviators; to secure the erection of a suitable monument by the U.S. Government and to sponsor an annual celebration at Kill Devil Hills on December 17 (First Flight Society pamphlet).

The Twenty-fifth Anniversary Celebration of the First Flight began on December 4, 1928, in Dayton, Ohio, with the laying of a commemorative wreath on Wilbur Wright's grave. Orville attended the International Civil Aeronautics Conference held in Washington, D.C. from December 12-14. The week was filled with many honors. One of them was the issuance of a two-cent United States postal stamp in commemoration of the Wright Flyer.

On December 16, two hundred distinguished guests boarded the steamer, *District of Columbia,* for their pilgrimage to Kitty Hawk. The trip started out poorly when fog delayed the departure. The travelers spent the night on board the steamer in Norfolk, Virginia. Buses arrived in the morning to transport the group across the North Carolina-Virginia border, down the Currituck peninsula to Currituck Sound. The road south was still a work in progress and eventually the buses were abandoned for cars, which ferried the travelers across log roads and mud to Point Harbor, where they boarded the ferry to cross the sound. Upon their arrival in Kitty Hawk, the visitors were transported by car to a luncheon prepared by the ladies of the county.

Just as high winds had provided added drama to the first flight, high winds provided a touch of realism to this first flight celebration. The beleaguered travelers trudged up the 100-foot sand dune to lay the corner stone. After speeches by Senator Bingham and the Secretary of Commerce, Dwight David, and the playing of the Star Spangled Banner, the group of distinguished visitors descended to the actual site of the first flight. The location of the site was determined by Captain William Tate, W. S. Dough, A.D. Etheridge and John Moore, all eye witnesses to the first manned flight on December 17,1903. Amelia Earhart, America's most famous aviatrix, unveiled the granite boulder, which marked the site.

CAPTAIN BILL TATE and ELIJAH BAUM

By the time that the sixty-one foot high pylon was completed in 1932 the road through lower Currituck County had been finished and the new Wright Memorial Bridge spanned Currituck Sound. But the weather was even more uncooperative than it had been in 1928. Cold rain poured down on those assembled and a gale force wind blew the canvas off the speaker's platform. Ruth Nichols unveiled the impressive monument and revealed the inscription:

**IN COMMEMORATION OF THE CONQUEST OF THE AIR
BY THE BROTHERS WILBUR AND ORVILLE WRIGHT
CONCEIVED BY
GENIUS
ACHIEVED BY DAUNTLESS RESOLUTION AND
UNCONQUERABLE FAITH**

WRIGHT BROTHERS NATIONAL MEMORIAL

ORVILLE WRIGHT AND THE WRIGHT FAMILY

This was the second monument constructed in Kitty Hawk. In 1928 William Tate and the citizens of Kitty Hawk had placed a marble marker on the spot where Wilbur assembled the 1900 glider. The original marker was damaged in a storm and was moved to a place of honor in the Kitty Hawk town hall. A duplicate marker still stands on Moore Shore Road. It is little known even by the current local residents.

Other monuments honor the two brothers from Dayton. One stands in a field in France where Wilbur first began his European flights. Another rests atop a hill overlooking Huffman Prairie outside Dayton. Orville received many honors on behalf of himself and his brother. But perhaps the most heartfelt honor came from the man who first welcomed them to Kitty Hawk in 1900, William Tate. On the occasion of the twenty-fifth anniversary, Tate said:

I am proud personally of my contact with the Wrights, that I lived to associate with them, and that I spent a good many of my loafing hours around their camp [. . .] I have paid many a tribute to them - Christian gentlemen. Moral to the core; nothing I can say can pay them too great a tribute (Proceedings, KDH, 1928, 24).

WILLIAM TATE GIVING HIS TRIBUTE TO THE WRIGHT BROTHERS

The honor which would have meant the most to Orville would have been to be present when the 1903 Wright Flyer was given a place of honor at the Smithsonian Institute. That honor was denied him.

On October 10, 1947, while hurrying to a meeting, Orville suffered his first heart attack. He was rushed to Dayton's Miami Hospital, but within a month was back at work in his office answering the many letters which had accumulated in his absence.

On the morning of January 27, he was busy fixing a broken doorbell, walking in and out of the cold and up and down the cellar steps. Later in the day he suffered his second heart attack. He was rushed to Miami Hospital. As sick as he was, he retained his sense of humor, requesting that Carrie Grumbach, his housekeeper, prepare his food. He told the nurse, "You had best let Carrie do that, Miss - she knows all my cranky little ways" (Howard 443).

Orville passed away quietly on Friday, January 30, 1948. On that day the world lost a truly great man. He and his brother changed the course of history. Whether the world chooses to use the Wrights' invention for its ultimate good or its ultimate failure is for the world to decide. Orville wrote in his lifetime:

I don't have any regrets about my part in the invention of the airplane, though no one, could deplore more than I do, the destruction it has caused. I feel about the airplane as I do in regard to fire. That is, I regret all the terrible damage caused by fire. But I think it is good for the human race that someone discovered how to start fires and it is possible to put fire to thousands of important uses (Jakab and Young 261).

ORVILLE WRIGHT

Bibliography

Albertson, Catherine. *Wings over Kill Devil and Legends of The Dunes of Dare.* Elizabeth City, N.C.: privately printed, 1928.

Brown, Aycock. *The Birth of Aviation: Kitty Hawk, NC.* Winston-Salem, NC: The Collins Company, 1953.

- - -. "On North Carolina's Banks." The News and Observer 16 May 1965.

Crouch, Tom. The Bishop's Boys: A Life of Wilbur and Orville Wright. New York: W.W. Norton & Company, 1989.

Culick, Fred E. C. and Spencer Dunmore. *On Great White Wings: The Wright Brothers and the Race for Flight.* New York, NY: Hyperion, 2001.

Durand, William F. "Biographical Memoir of Orville Wright." Paper: National Academy of Sciences Vol. XXV. 1948.

"The Failure of Langley's Aerodrome." Scientific American October 1903: 272+. <http://invention.psychology.msstate.edu/library/magazines/langley-f...>

"Flights of Inspiration." First Flight: Parts I, II, III, IV. British Science Museum. <http://www/sciencemuseum.org.uk/on-line/flights/first/into.asp.>

Fisk, Fred C. and Marlin W. Todd. The Wright Brothers from Bicycle to Biplane. Dayton, Ohio: Fisk & Todd, 2000.

Geibert, Ronald R. and Patrick B. Nolan. *Kitty Hawk and Beyond.* Dayton, Ohio: Wright State University Press, 1990.

Gibbs-Smith, Charles H. *The Wright Brothers.* London: Her Majesty's Stationery Office, 1963.

Glass, Jon. "Soaring Tales of the First Flight." The North Carolina Coast Dec. 17, 1987: Vol 2, 71.

Hallion, Richard P. *The Wright Brothers: Heirs to Prometheus.* Washington, DC: Smithsonian Press, 1978.

Harris, Bill. Personal interview with the author, October, 2002

"History of Flight from Around the World." American Institute of Aeronautics and Astronautics. <http://www.flight100.org/history/timeline.cfm?period=2000s>

Howard, Fred. Wilbur and Orville Wright: A Biography of the Wright Brothers. Mineola, NY: Dover Publications, 1998.

Jakab, Peter L. and Rick Young. *The Published Writings of Wilbur and Orville Wright.* Washington, DC: Smithsonian Press, 1990.

Jones, LuAnne and Amy Glass. *"Everyone Helped His Neighbor": Memories of Nags Head Woods.* Nags Head Woods Oral History Project. 1986.

Kelly, Fred. Miracle at Kitty Hawk: The Letters of Wilbur and Orville Wright. New York: Da Capo Press. 1996.

- - -. *The Wright Brothers*: New York: Dover Publications Inc., 1989

Kidder, Chris. *Aloft At Last: How the Wright Brothers Made History.* Nags Head, NC: Nags Head Art, Inc., 2002.

Kirk, Stephen. *First in Flight: The Wright Brothers in North Carolina.* Winston-Salem, NC: John F. Blair Publisher, 1995.

McFarland, Marvin R. *The Papers of Wilbur and Orville Wright*. Salem, NY: Ayer Co., 1990.

McMahon, John R. *The Wright Brothers*. New York: Grosset & Dunlap, 1930.

Mouillard, Louis-Pierre. Cosmopolitan February 1894: 459+. <http://invention.psychology.msstate.edu/library/magazines/mouillar...>

Newcomb, Simon. "Is The Airship Coming?" McClure's Magazine 17 Sept., 1901, 432-435. <http://invention.psychology.msstate.edu/library/Magazines/Airship...>

Oliver, Mary. "Hawthorn Hill: The Wright Family Home." Symposium Paper: Following the Footsteps of the Wright Brothers: Dayton, Ohio, Sept. 23, 2001. <http://www.libraries.wright.edu/special/symposium/oliver.html#study.>

"Recent French Aeroplanes and Their Performances." Scientific American Jan. 1909:81+. <http://invention.psychology.msstate.edu//library/Magazines/ParisAer...>

Sanford, John. "The First Aerial Canoe: Wilbur Wright and the Hudson-Fulton Flights." Symposium Paper: Following The Footsteps of the Wright Brothers. Dayton,Ohio:2002. <http://www.libraries.wright.edu/special/symposium/sanford.html.>

Stick, David. *The Outer Banks of North Carolina*. Chapel Hill, NC: University of North Carolina Press, 1958.

Tate, William J. "With the Wrights at Kitty Hawk." Aeronautic Review Dec. 1928: 29-36.

"The Wright Aeroplane and Its Performances." Scientific American April 1904: 291+. <http://invention.psychology.msstate.edu/i/wrights/library/wright-si...>

"The Wright Aeroplane and Its Fabled Performances." Scientific American Jan. 1905: 40+. <http://invention.psychology.msstate.edu/i/wrights/library/wright-si...>

Wright, Milton. *Diaries 1857-1917*. Dayton, Ohio: Wright State University Press, 1999.

Wright Brothers Official Map and Guide. Wright Brothers National Memorial, Kill Devil Hills, NC: National Park Service, GPO, 2000.

Wright, Orville. *How We Invented The Airplane*. Edited with commentary by Fred Kelly. New York: McKay 1953.

_ _ _"The Wright Brothers Aeroplane." Century Magazine Sept. 1908. <http://invention.psychology. msstate.edu/i/Wright/library/Century.html>

Wright, Orville and Wilbur Wright. *O.& W. Flying Machine: Patent, No. 821, 393*.Washington,D.C.:May22,1906. <http://invention.psychology.msstate.edu/i/Wrights/WrightUSPatent.>

Young, Rosamond and Catherine Fitzgerald. *Twelve Seconds To The Moon: Story of The Wright Brothers*. Second edition. Dayton, Ohio: U. S. Air Force Foundation, 1983.

INDEX

A TALE OF TWO BROTHERS

Order Information

Trafford Publishing

Suite 6E 2333 Government St. Victoria, BC., Canada V8T 4P4

Phone 250-383-6864 Toll-free 1-888-232-4444 (Canada & US)

Fax 250-383-6864 Email info@trafford.com

Website www.trafford.com

****

OR

Judith A. Dempsey (author)
Post Office Box 210, Kitty Hawk, NC, 27949

Fax 252-261-6599 E-mail obxosprey@cs.com